God & Soul Theory

Edward Conklin Ph.D.

Edward Conklin

Copyright 2019 by Edward Conklin. All Rights Reserved.

This book or any portion thereof may not be reproduced or used in any manner including any electronic or mechanical information storage and retrieval systems, without the express permission of the publisher. Scanning, uploading, photocopying, and facilitating the electronic distribution of this book without permission of the publisher is prohibited.

ISBN 978-0-9988338-5-9

Edward Conklin

Dedication

I dedicate this work to the curious and brave few, those of the past who have, and those of the future who will make the effort to peer beneath the surface of things, and to better comprehend life and death and who will share what they find with others. I also dedicate this work to the young, who not told, usually must find out the hard way.

Edward Conklin

Acknowledgments

To parents and family generations I owe my biological life. I acknowledge and especially thank my religious mother and pagan father who provided a contrast of values and also a sufficient amount of both comfort and discomfort to influence my early years. I acknowledge my teacher, Dr. Amiya Chakravarty (1901-1986) who contributed to my philosophical orientation in life. Words fail to adequately convey my heartfelt appreciation for his guidance, and for inspiring me to think more deeply about the human condition.

Edward Conklin

Published works by Edward Conklin Ph.D.

God & Soul Theory. (2019). Amazon Kindle and Paperback Edition.

Original Sin: A God-Soul Theory. (2018). Amazon Kindle and Paperback Edition.

God-Soul Theory for the 21st Century. (2017). Amazon Kindle and Paperback Edition.

Psychology of God and the Soul. (2016). Amazon Kindle and Paperback Edition.

Meditations on God and the Soul. (2015). Amazon Kindle and Paperback Edition.

A Brief Guide to God and the Soul. (2015). Amazon Kindle and Paperback Edition.

In the Beginning: A New Theory of the First Religion. (2014). Amazon Kindle and Paperback Edition.

Cosmos, God, and Soul. (2014). Amazon Kindle and Paperback Edition.

From Tool-maker to God Maker. (2014). Amazon Kindle and Paperback Edition.

Waves Rough and Smooth & the Deep Blue Sea. (2014). Amazon Kindle and Paperback Edition.

Getting Back Into the Garden of Eden. (1998). University Press of America.

Edward Conklin

Table of Contents

Introduction	Good and Bad News
Search	Front Man
Inductive Reasoning	First Father
Pragmatic Truth	Ruler
First Religion	Metaphorical
Knowledge	Metaphysical
Tool	Laying Down the Burden
Word Art	Soul
Cocoon	Save
Graven Image	Cerebral God
Genesis	Problem of Willing
Care	Addiction
Garden of Eden	Monotheistic Willing
Slave	God and Human Will
Good Knowledge	Das Ville
Sex	Pragmatic Willing
Poor Priests	Existence
Sheepish	Supplement
God & Soul Theory and Jesus	Ever Changing
Guide to Good	Habit Pattern
Poetic Musing	Willing Groove
Refuge	Spirit and Soul
Mess	Self and Soul
Zoroastrianism	Difference
Alma Mater	Relief
Bright Spot	Curse
Fortification	Life Remedy
Help	Willing
First Father Willing	Dynamic
Rational	Reinforcement
Story	Company
Special	Error
Great	Insurance Policy
Worth	Ally
Separation	Meditation

Clarity
Subject
Meditative Attention
Enlightenment
Survival
Wrestling
Retreat
Poise
Breath of Life
Words
Order
Order and Disorder
Lower to Higher
Pleasure
Garden of Eden
Buddha
Good and Evil Fruit
Real Exodus
Soul Day
European Soul
Praise
Soulless
Soulless Versus Soul
Soul Musing
Trouble
Shunning
Garden Growth
Cultivate Your Garden
Life Lesson
Soulish
Soul Litter
Cleanup
Undo
Meditation and Dissociation
Urges and Images
Misplace
Trick

Seductive
Offer
Stability
Two Legends
Autism Spectrum Disorder
Advantage
Subjective Story
Human Willing
Alias
Eyes
Atheism
Superstition
Fresh Water

Introduction

This work is a discussion on the existence of a monotheistic god and a human soul. The God & Soul Theory asserts that monotheistic authorities and their many followers, are mere aficionados of the cerebral cortex of the brain, the only place where the idea of a first father is located. Unfortunately for humankind, a first father god does not exist objectively but only as a subjective artistic work of word art. Monotheistic religions rely on faith, belief, and tradition as superficial rationale for the objective existence of a first father god. For science, the existence of a monotheistic god is subjective superstition.

Monotheistic religions are soulless religions as they do not accept the existence of an animating soul. Monotheistic religions accept that humans have a spirit or breath and a free will but these functions are viewed as mortal as is the body, and following death can only be someday resurrected by a first father god. The God & Soul Theory advocates for the real existence of a human soul and that it is a triune dynamic of a hunger for food and water, sex and reproduction, and aggression. As a continuation of a seething sea of natural energy particles of the environment, the soul is resistant to destruction.

Science considers the existence of an animating soul to be superstition. The scientific insistence on observation of the human soul is met by the God & Soul Theory but to test for its existence is not a proper format. Time will tell whether the God & Soul Theory will make a meaningful contribution to a better comprehension of a monotheistic god and a human soul. The task may take a while as the words of theoretical physicist Max Planck (1858-1947) suggest:

"A new truth does not triumph by convincing its opponents and making them see the light, but rather its opponents eventually die, and a new generation grows up that is familiar with it."

The best way around outdated beliefs and ideas is to avoid those who over zealously defend them. The generations of the future will be less prejudicial and defensive, and more open to weighing the evidence for the propositions of the God & Soul Theory.

The God & Soul Theory must compete for attention in the marketplace of ideas and theories, especially against monotheistic religions, the busy babble of daily news, fiction literature, and an inane and often borderline meaningless media of magazines, internet, television, and cinema. If by chance an inquisitive individual might spare some time to investigate what the God & Soul Theory has to say, the reader will be rewarded with a much-improved comprehension of a first father god, the soul, and humankind's profound place in a natural and preternatural universe.

It is rewarding to contribute the propositions of the God & Soul Theory to the long-held human discussion about the existence of a monotheistic god. It is even more uplifting to contribute to the discussion of what has long been of interest to many and yet has remained shrouded in vagueness and mystery, the human soul.

Search

Life is a busy search for pleasure or relief from pain of many kinds. In the continual back and forth shuttle of change, most people lack sufficient time and fail to search for a better comprehension of life. Many people fall into comfortable or uncomfortable routines of family and social life, work, and accumulating the necessities and pragmatic knowledge required for daily existence. Only a minority of a population conduct a search for and succeed in acquiring what is truly valuable in life, namely health, knowledge, work and financial security, and supportive relationships. Far too many people accept superficial beliefs and traditions, and few conduct a search to better comprehend the origin of life and death. Even fewer manage a search to comprehend brain and body functions, and to comprehend the conscious human self and the less conscious and subconscious soul.

Much of life is a word game. Words are pragmatically useful to refer to and describe real events occurring in the environment and life experience. Words are also used to refer to and describe what is only a subjective image in the cerebral cortex of the brain, such as the fictional characters of a unicorn, the tooth fairy, and Santa Claus. A monotheistic god unquestionably belongs in the latter category.

A question long been asked is, does a monotheistic god who made the environment and life exist? The God & Soul Theory answer to the question is, yes, a first father does exist subjectively in the cerebral cortex of the human brain but does not exist objectively at any other location. A monotheistic god is a subjectively imagined parental model utilized to orient and to identify the beginning of existence and to direct attention to where care and protection can be obtained through petitionary prayer. A subjectively conceived first father god serves for many as a helping and protective ideational umbrella during the expected and unexpected storms of daily life.

A monotheistic god is only half real as it exists as a subjective imaginal idea in the cerebral cortex of the brain but does not exist objectively. The God & Soul Theory argues for a psychological view of partial atheism.

The theory asserts that a monotheistic god is an expression of human ability for artistic ideation and word art. A monotheistic god is a prescientific and subjective way of identifying the origin of existence and is an artistic spoken and written word portrait orientation to what is good and protective of humans. The first father of monotheistic religions is derived not from reasoning but is a product of artistic imagining, the making of images in a word story in an effort to identify an unknown beginning of the environment and life. A monotheistic god is an acceptable idea to a sizeable number of humans but the acceptance, faith, belief, and tradition of many people furnishes no reliable assurance that it is objectively real.

Stories about a monotheistic god impress many people but few like to hear remarks that a monotheistic god does not exist. A monotheistic god is a subjectively imagined helper for those who lack help and hope. To say to these individuals a first father god does not exist, is to increase feelings of existential angst, helplessness, hopelessness, and anger. Humans make mistakes, have accidents, illnesses, and consequently experience difficulty getting through daily life that occurs against a sensed background of a vast cosmic space and seeming endless time. When encountering existential angst and confusion, a person will quickly turn to any help that is offered, regardless if it happens to be subjectively ideated and imagined help of a monotheistic god. For individuals who lack the ability to succeed, lack assistance from fellow humans, and are depressed and desperate, an imagined first father companion is the only help available and a last resort.

A subjectively imagined monotheistic god represents the intelligence of the cerebral cortex of the human brain, while the role of first father represents the beginning of a long line of biological reproduction. The conscious cerebral cortex of the brain imagines, meaning, it makes an ideational image of a first father god as a way of directing and controlling the nonresponsive environment and the human subconscious functions of the midbrain and body behaviors. The subjectively imagined and externalized monotheistic god is an explanation for a real internal animation of life.

This leads to another important question humans have long asked, is there a soul within the body that survives physical death? While popularly referred to, it has been difficult for humans to comprehend and to define what a soul is except to say it survives death. The separating sin of monotheistic religions is the nonattention to a real animating soul, and instead a directing of attention to the word art of a first father god who is the only animator of the body. Monotheistic religions are soulless and insist that humans have a living body, (Hebrew *nefesh*) an animating breath (Hebrew *ruach*) or spirit, (Latin *spiritus*) and a free will, each of which are mortal. The monotheistic religions of Judaism, Christianity, and Islam, are soulless and instead rely on a resurrection of the physical body. Therefore, the popular yet poorly conceived notion of a human soul cannot have been made by and has nothing to do with the first father god of monotheism.

An animating soul is a continuation of real energy particles of the earth and sun environment and it is this factor that renders it resistant to destruction. Monotheistic religions ignore that life is a continuation of the environment, and instead ideate and artistically portray the word portrait of a first father god to be the exclusive origin of existence. By directing attention externally to a god, monotheistic followers fail to direct and focus attention to what animates life internally. What internally exists to grow and evolve life is a continuation of and is supported by the environment. A first father god is a subjective conceived idea with which to manage the external environment and is utilized to socially govern internal willful human behaviors, especially of hunger for food, sex and reproduction, and aggression.

To look at the earth is to see the real relative and external origin of life. To observe the dynamic of hunger for food and water, sex and reproduction, and aggression is to look at the real internal origin of life, the triune soul. To better comprehend this three-strand dynamic of life is to unravel the mysterious origin of existence. The soul is a real trinity, a triune dynamic continuation of energy that is resistant to destruction. The soul enables an individual to survive daily life, and as some evidence suggests, continues to survive physical death.

Inductive Reasoning

The experimental method of science, the manipulation of independent and dependent variables during a test experiment is a useful tool, and one of many to be utilized in seeking what is true. Test results provide data from which a conclusion can be drawn and a probable theory generated. While providing reliable evidence for a conclusion and theory, the experimental method of laboratory research is not the only criterion of what is true. Reliable conclusions can also be reached based on observing repetitive behaviors in a natural setting. With observation of behaviors, inductive reasoning can be used to arrive at a reliable and probable conclusion as to correlation. Repeated observations of behavior over time, can like experimental methodology, yield a conclusion and a theory based on what is probably true.

The God & Soul Theory is based on observation and inductive reasoning. A phenomenological methodology of meditative effort and daily practice was implemented to improve cognitive clarity by reducing attention to sensations and excess picture mages, and by close observation of the general dynamic of brain and body functions. Through observation and intuitive comprehension, a monotheistic god can be better recognized for what it really is, a simple subjective ideation creatively placed in a cobbled together artistic story of word art. Based on numerous observations and use of inductive reasoning, this assertion becomes obvious and convincing.

Using observation and inductive reasoning, a conclusion about the animating of life can also be drawn. When conscious attention is focused and not distracted by sensations and picture images or thoughts, and sleep does not occur, three dynamic drives or urges within the human body become noticeably prominent. These are the dynamic biological urges of hunger for food and water, sex and reproduction, and aggression that are correlated with survival. Supported by numerous observations over many years, the inductive conclusion reached is that this triune dynamic is the previous undefined, unrecognized, and long sought for human soul.

Pragmatic Truth

The average person is generally interested in finding what is true. Members of the legal system and scientists specialize in searching for objective truths. Not included are authorities and advocates of monotheistic religions who do not value real and objective truth. A monotheistic god is a popular pragmatic truth that is based on subjective faith, trust, and tradition. The promotion and acceptance of a monotheistic god to be objective is quite frankly a fraud, as a first father exists only as a subjective artistic work of spoken and written word art. That a first father of all fathers is a completely subjective idea, is evident by the fact that monotheistic religions rely on faith (Latin *fidere*, trust) and do not insist on finding or detecting objective evidence of the god. The usual explanation for not objectively seeking the first father is that it is not visible, or the god appears only to a deserving person, or to a rare saintly individual and not to average people.

Monotheistic authorities and their followers would not even be interested in searching for the objective existence of a first father god and would consider the quest to be a waste of time. In fact, those who advocate for a monotheistic god, whether sacerdotalists or adherents, stridently insist the existence of a first father must be accepted only on faith and trust and not to look for signs. The lack of insistence on objective evidence for the existence of a first father, convincingly suggests that a monotheistic first father god is a total subjective fabrication.

The worship of a monotheistic god is a simple subjective way for individuals to wrap themselves with protection. Directing attention to a first father, members of monotheistic religions ensconce themselves in the imagined care and protection of a god who directs attention back to them. Wishful faith in a metaphysical monotheistic god is pragmatically useful for an average individual to simplistically identify the origin of existence. A first father is a simple axiom that does not involve a great deal of investigation and comprehension, only faith, belief, and tradition.

Monotheism is a lazy person's religion, for nonthinkers and those who fail to question and investigate. The artistic word portrait of a first father god avoids a real examination of what internally animates life and its dynamic dependence on and origin from the environment.

First Religion

Artifact evidence suggests that Paleolithic homo sapiens, circa 40,000-10,000 BCE, conceived and compared the earth to be a female origin of animal and human life. In France and Spain, early humans artistically drew and painted animals on cave walls to petition and assist the earth to bring the figures to life and send them to be hunted and harvested for food to sustain living.

This artistic practice is some of the earliest artifact evidence for the existence of religion. Influenced by this early religious behavior, all later religions have artistically imagined and visually, verbally, or wrote word story portraits about various gods. That is all any religion is, a creative product, an expression of artistic impulse and imaginal words that convey a spoken or written story. The human creative process of god-making is subjective and artistic and is certainly not a realistic, mathematical, or scientific effort to objectively comprehend reality.

During times of need, individuals seek help, care, and protection. Paleolithic peoples sought help from what they conceived to be the origin of life, the earth which they depended on to provide shelter and food. In historic times, if help cannot be obtained from the environment or other humans, it can be subjectively imagined and obtained through acceptance of a written genealogical word portrait of a monotheistic god. Individuals can then seek to gain the attention of a first father, and can then be favored. The person can petition for assistance to accomplish goals and to receive more knowledge from the intelligent god. The human ego occurs in the conscious cerebral cortex of the brain, precisely where the alter ego of a monotheistic god is ideated. Ego begets ego and real little human egos follow a subjective ideated bigger ego of a first father god.

Monotheism solves the problem of an unknown beginning by assigning the personality of a first father god. Monotheistic religions poorly solve the difficulty of where existence comes from by imagining and writing stories about a god that also represents what is good, caring, and protective of humans. Monotheistic religions further solve the problem of evil by merely assigning another personality. Just as a first father is an artistic ideated good, so is Satan, Devil, Lucifer, and Iblis an imagined evil.

Knowledge

The biblical Genesis story of a monotheistic god who makes the environment and life, represents an imaginative artistic wish by the conscious cerebral cortex of the human brain to identify the origin of existence. A first father is the subjective way the cerebral brain knows the beginning of existence, how it can vicariously control the environment, and is a way to direct human attention to what is good in a dual good and evil life existence. Biblical word artists extrapolate human origin from many biological forefathers and exaggerate them to be a first father and a super god. Utilizing subjective ideation, the word artist scribes artistically valorized their vulnerable biological existence.

Onto the local and nonlocal panorama of reality experience, artist storytellers of the primitive past projected subjective story knowledge of a fantastic first father to be the willing cause of the environment and life. Modern humans who seek reliable knowledge of the origin of existence must look to the findings of science and not to vaunted faith in the word art story of a monotheistic god. The subjective notion of an intelligent first father is often pragmatically useful. Unfortunately, many otherwise intelligent people do not bother to investigate or to comprehend that a monotheistic god is a psychological construct and artistic work of spoken and written word art.

Tool

All tools are useful but eventually with time become worn, and may be repaired but eventually have to be discarded. Middle East cultures pragmatically fabricated, and Western countries have accepted through the years, the subjective artistic tool of a monotheistic god. A first father is utilized as a way to identify human origin, and to assist humans to fit in and feel more comfortable with each other and with the changing environment. Like all tools that are worn, broken, and no longer useful, the subjective tool of a monotheistic god must also eventually be discarded. Over use through time have caused the subjective tool of a first father to weaken, become worn, and barely usable, and is no longer a reliable way to comprehend existence.

Biblical authors of the book of Genesis artistically ideated a superior intelligence that existed prior to humans, a first father who brought the environment, life, and humankind into existence. A monotheistic god is a written word portrait utilized to identify the origin of the environment and life, and especially the cultural group. A first father is an artistic representation of what really brought humans into existence, a genealogy of many previous and barely intelligent biological fathers and mothers engaging in sexual reproduction.

Many adherents deem a monotheistic god to be the only good in a dual good and evil existence. The only genuine real small good of life is the barely intelligent cerebral cortex of the evolved human brain. Prior to scientific knowledge, the cerebral cortex used its artistic ability to imagine, to make images of story and to represent human origin by sketching the word portrait character of a monotheistic god. Early human intelligence was not able to comprehend the origin of the environment and life to be energy, and instead opted for the simple story of a first father god.

An imagined first father and god story was necessary circa 500 BCE as it was not possible for monotheistic writers of Genesis to comprehend that human life is animated by an internal soul that is a continuation of the external environment. Much of the evil of existence is the external changing will-like environment while the internal evil is an animating soul. The soul is a triune willing of urges as hunger for food and water, sex and reproduction, and aggression.

A monotheistic god is a subjective refuge from the external environment and from an internal troubling, unruly, and disobedient soul.

Word Art

The human brain is innately artistic. From sensations of the senses, the evolved cerebral cortex makes internal picture images of external objects in conscious attention. The external objects exist as images in a mental space and time. Mimicking this innate process, humans like to behaviorally make representations of objects known as art, including visual painting and sculptures, the notes of sound known as music, and the word art of verbal or written story.

The writings of monotheistic religions are subjective works of word art. In the past, the only way to know the origin of existence was to tell or write a story about it. Straining to comprehend the origin of existence, the cerebral cortex of early biblical writers furnished an artistic answer to the question of where the environment and life comes from by imagining and writing down stories of a first father. The story of a monotheistic god is an artistic word portrait, a verbal and written illustration of the origin of existence. By continuing to accept and prefer the story of a first father god to be the origin of existence, many modern humans continue to wander through a storyland maze of monotheistic word art and its many circuitous byways of good and evil.

Monotheistic authorities continue to convince the under-educated and gullible of a population to accept an artistic spoken and written word portrait of a first father god. Sacerdotalists make a living helping the helpless and hopeless by rendering assistance, charity, and advice. Sacerdotalists also offer hapless individuals the artistic word portrait of a monotheistic god. If the word art of a first father is accepted, the individual can then subjectively rely on the god to help them. The idea of a first father who has a strong will is pitched as an offer of help to an individual. If accepted, the idea has some negligible placebo effect to reinforce weaker or subpar individual willing with subjective hope.

The authors of the Genesis story utilized word art to make known a genealogical beginning by a first father. This was a simplistic and artistic way of identifying where the environment and life comes from. Following this tradition, monotheistic sacerdotalists help themselves to a way of making a living by providing the pablum word art story of a first father helper who helps humans. Their work is to convince those who would listen that a monotheistic god is a helpful way to overcome the helpless situations of life and death. The word art portrait of a good first father god is a help to many, as it diverts attention away from the not so good experiences of life. Directing attention to a good first father is a way of making life more tolerable by indulging in prayer, and perhaps routine weekly group worship rituals, so as to maintain or regain equilibrium from the unexpected and upsetting situations and experiences of life.

The word art sketch of a greater good god origin also helps to encourage individuals to do good and to refrain from acts of excessive force or evil. The existence of a monotheistic god directs human attention and willing to good behaviors with an expectation of reward and away from willing bad behaviors and expected punishment.

A monotheistic god story is a subjective artistic strain of the brain, the cerebral cortex, to identify an unknown beginning. A first father is a subjective artistic idea of the brain that makes use of spoken and written words arranged on the pages of a scroll or book. A monotheistic god is a strain of the brain as it is an artistic effort to imagine, to make an image of the origin of existence by describing it with words of a story. A first father god is merely an artistic genealogy ideationally portrayed in word art of story and pandered to the credulous as credible and worthy of acceptance.

In the biblical Genesis story, the material earth is portrayed as not able to develop life on its own. Generally, circa 500 BCE, aside from bringing forth plant life, the soil was considered as inert. Besides, only what is humanlike can make humans. In the Garden of Eden story, a first father ancestor scooped up some soil from the earth and shaped it into the first human. (Genesis 2:7)

Today it is known the earth is not inert but is composed of reactive energy particles, elements, and minerals that actively form and support the chemistry of evolving life. A monotheistic god is a subjective superficial idea that represents what was unknown at the time, a real essence of animating energy particles. The organizing of life occurs internally as a continuation and dependent function of external supportive energy particles of the sun and earth environment.

Cocoon

Middle East word artists must have reached a limit of frustration of not being able to know the origin of existence, and probably reached a limit of disgust with many coarse, uncaring, and aggressive human behaviors. To remedy the two existential situations, biblical word artists wrote a word portrait of a monotheistic god to describe the genesis of existence and to serve as a pragmatic aid to direct human behavior.

The Genesis word artists spun for themselves a metaphorical cocoon as a subjective way to identify their cultural origin and to provide care and protection. Ever since, the analogical cocoon of a monotheistic god has served as a shelter for needy caterpillars everywhere. Over the past two thousand years, the monotheistic cocoon culture has spread to western cultures. Fortunately, Asian cultures have resisted the caterpillar cocoon invasion of monotheism. Today, convert caterpillars continue to read and feed upon the sustenance leaved pages of monotheistic scriptures and literature. The spun chrysalis or sheltering cocoon of a first father god continues to serve as a camouflage refuge of words, a subjective way to protect those who take shelter within it from the potential dangers and harms of the real environment and the aggressive behaviors of fellow humans.

Contemporary caterpillars continue the tradition to reside in the confines of the constructed word-built cocoon of monotheism and its first father god at the cost of not maturing into an adult butterfly. To live in a word-spun cocoon and not continue to evolve and explore outside of its limiting belief and tradition, is an intellectual failure.

The sheltering cocoon is a barrier to exiting its pragmatic and once needed limiting confines. To remain within the cocoon at the cost of individual flight and exploration of the greater inner and outer environment, is a sacrifice of real and reliable knowledge to the ogre of limiting blind faith, belief, and empty tradition.

The task of humankind is to break through and exit the shelter of the monotheistic word concocted cocoon, and to take a risk and brave the individual flight of life experience in acquiring knowledge. To insist on remaining sheltered in a protective cocoon of words about a monotheistic god, retards personal growth and unfoldment, whereby the ability for freedom of flight is handicapped and eventually atrophied. To live confined in a cocoon of words is a life both limited and stifled.

Many people choose not to leave the confines of the monotheistic refuge, and shelter in place to live a limiting lifestyle of comprehension, marooned in an arrested developmental stage of a word-built cocoon. Surely, some caterpillars must have an evolutionary sense that the cocoon of protection is a temporary construct and humankind cannot always remain within it. Curious caterpillars will one day have to exit the makeshift shelter during a sensed impending transformation and independent flight. Eventually, the word-built cocoon of a monotheistic god will no longer be needed by humankind to serve as a subjective shelter from the objective challenges of living and dying.

Graven Image

The second of the biblical ten commandments (Exodus 20:4-6; Deuteronomy 5:8) dictated by a monotheistic first father is to not represent the god as a "graven image" or idol (Hebrew *pesel*). The prohibition by the god is also mentioned in the book of Leviticus.

"Ye shall make you no idols nor graven image, neither rear you up a standing image, neither shall ye set up any image of stone in your land, to bow down to it: for I am the Lord your God." (Leviticus 26:1)

Idols are images cut, carved, incised, or engraved into a desired shape. The first father god of monotheism is not portrayed as a standing image sculpted with stone, metal, or wood but is only allowed by scribal authorities to be graven with spoken and written words impressed on memory and illustrated with words on parchment or paper. The verb to grave means:

"To engrave, stamp, or impress deeply or firmly in conscious attention and memory, to etch a design, or to write letters or words on a surface."

In the Tanak or Old Testament, words are inscribed to describe the behaviors of a monotheistic god. The origin of existence as told in the book of Genesis, is a first father represented with graven letters and words shaped and gravened into story images of a word art portrait. In the Genesis story, biblical writers idolize with words a first father as an all-powerful god and this adulation is in violation of the later second commandment. Chapter 1 of the book of Genesis remarks that everything the first father made was "good." This praise is an idolizing of the subjectively imagined first father who is also a god. When monotheistic word artist scribes and adherents imagine and uncritically praise the origin of existence to be a first father and a god, they are idolizing it.

To idolize is to engage in "a blind or uncritical admiration and devotion," in this case a first father. There is uncritical acceptance and little or no questioning or appraisal of the god's behaviors or commandments. A monotheistic god is a subjective work of spoken and written word art, a graven image of story that requires faith and belief in its existence. Monotheistic word art that details the adventures of a first father is an artistic idolization of genealogy, and as such the character represents the sexual orgasm and reproduction of many forefathers.

In a vain attempt to avoid making a graven image, the Hebrew word *hashem* (the name) is used as a substitute when Jews write the name of the god Yhwh, or may leave the name incomplete such as Y--h.

The real or full name of the god is avoided as to say it evokes closeness and familiarity with the special first father. Speaking or writing the full name of the god also takes on an uncomfortable meaning of a representation, idol, or graven image. Yet, the stories of the first father consist of a description and graven word images of the god doing and speaking. Any mention in story of the monotheistic god is a graven image, an imaginal likeness portrayed with words. A monotheistic god is a graven image of words and as a mental idol endures through tradition.

Erecting the word built idol of a first father god is an artistic way to identify the origin of existence. While so doing, the idol also obscures and makes it difficult to perceive an animating soul to be the essential vital function of life. The story of a first father is a failure of comprehension of what animates life, the external environment and an internal soul. Imagined by word artist scribes, a god covers over the real animation of life by a soul that is a continuation of energy particles of the earth and sun environment. Monotheistic word art of an idolized first father god is based on ignorance of a real genealogy from the outer environment and the inner dynamic of an animating and willing triune soul. The Genesis word story is an adulating of the conscious self of the cerebral cortex, alias the first father god, over an innate animating and willing triune soul of life. The soul dynamic is the less conscious and subconscious midbrain and body urges to survive as hunger for food and water, sex and reproduction, and aggression.

Genesis

Circa 600-500 BCE in the Middle East, a few word artist scribes sat down to write and to later edit a word portrait story of a first father and idolized it to be a monotheistic god. The writers crafted a story of the beginning of existence, explained why humans suffer in life, and a genealogy was also included. By accepting the existence of a monotheistic god, adherents claim to share a mutual origin and are related to others who accept the genealogy. Genesis chapters 4, 5 and 11 mention the Judaic genealogies.

Two later genealogies of Jesus are mentioned in the gospels, Matthew 1:17 and Luke 3:23-38. In Luke 3:28, Adam is listed as the son of the god who is listed first in the genealogy. Therefore, the god is regarded as a first father of humans. Genesis chapters 16 and 21, tell the story of Abraham, Hagar, and Ishmael to which the adherents of Islam trace their genealogy.

Looking at the Genesis story and its genealogy, the family story of Jesus, and the lineage of Islam, it is evident there has been a dysfunctional familial conflict of egos from the beginning. Yet, monotheistic adherents take on the task of convincing others that if only they join the family of the first father god and become good brothers and sisters by only willing good and not evil, then all will be well with humankind. Using the past as a guide, there is little likelihood of this ever happening.

The book of Genesis chapter 1 extolls the harmony and function of an overall interdependent and good existence, including an approval of sex and reproduction. (1:28) In contrast, chapter 2 is a closer look at the real dynamic of life, what it truly is versus what is glossed over in chapter 1. In Genesis chapters 2 to 4, the dynamic of life is exposed to be what it really is, a good and evil struggle for food and water, sex and reproduction, and aggression. In chapter 1, the monotheistic god gave humans a hunger for food and told them to multiply, not mathematically but sexually (Genesis 1:28-30) In chapter 2, there is not only hunger for food but also a hunger of the cerebral cortex for knowledge, especially of the origin of existence and for care and protection. The hunger for knowledge of the beginning by artist scribes was so great it produced the word portrait of a first father of many fathers, and was exalted to be a god. An existential hunger to know the origin of existence was slaked by word artist scribes who penned creative images of story to satisfy their own and the mass cultural appetite to comprehend the origin of the human condition.

The cultural word idol of a monotheistic god erected in the past by a few Middle East word artist scribes, continues to be gullibly accepted by later generations.

Like the subjective word art stories of Santa Claus, Easter bunny, giants, dragons, and mermaids, so too is the imaginative theological word art portrait of a monotheistic god. To objectively represent the origin of life in modern times, it is far better to utilize a rounded model of the earth, sun, atoms and electrons, and space to represent a real cosmological origin. A theological genesis is simple word art, while a geological origin is real and true.

Care

For biblical word artists, it was not acceptable for the origin of the universe to remain unknown or to be uncaring. The beginning of existence was then to be known and artistically portrayed with spoken and written words to be a monotheistic god. A first father god is an artistic use of story to locate the origin of existence and is a way to obtain care in a noncaring environment and among uncaring humans.

Biblical word artists wrote a fictional story to identify the origin of existence and the tale continues to provide many individuals with a subjective feeling of care. It seems there is little care available in existence as even the first father has a poor record of caring. In the Genesis story, the monotheistic god is portrayed as caring for the first humans by making a good and safe Garden of Eden. The Genesis first father soon became angry and refused to care for the first humans and banished them to care for themselves. The absence of personal interaction with and care by the first father for humans, is explained to be punishment by the god. The first humans used their free will made by the first father to disobey and the god ceased to care for and refused to allow them to reside in a place of care and protection. Ever since, the god only occasionally provides care to individuals, or shows attention by punishing them.

Most often, the god has ceased to care and to intervene in the lives of humans who are so often burdened by many troubling cares, despair, and suffering. To imagine a first father of many previous fathers, and to exaggerate it into the word art portrait story of a god, is a delusion or mistaken idea that comforts many.

Faith, belief, and tradition in the existence of a monotheistic god is a blind acceptance of what only exists subjectively and with spoken and written words. Earthly fathers may not do such a good job of caring for family, friends, and fellow humans but a first father of all fathers must surely care.

If an individual subjectively accepts that they are cared for by a monotheistic god, then the person does not need to spend a lot of time being overly careful or worrying about what will happen next in life or death. A monotheistic god is a symptom of an individual inability to adequately care for their own life and death. Humans have a difficult time during life to take care of themselves, and therefore, many respond by accepting the origin of existence to be the caring personality of a monotheistic god. A first father is a subjective and unrealistic way some humans care for themselves. Rather than depend on a god, each individual must learn to realistically care about their own health, knowledge, work and financial security, and obtaining care and loving support of family and friends.

Rather than wasting time caring about the subjective artistic word portrait of a monotheistic god, it is better for humans to care about directing attention to, observing, exploring, and comprehending a real human self and soul. The two terms of god and soul, are antagonistic to each other in meaning. A monotheistic god is only imagined to exist externally while a real soul exists internally.

Garden of Eden

In the biblical Genesis story, the first humans willfully disobeyed the first father and in so doing separated themselves from him. (Chapter 3) The god then banished the prototype humans from his paradisiacal Garden of Eden. This event is accepted by Christians to be the original sin of human separation from the monotheistic good god. The Garden story is an artistic metaphor that represents a real separation of higher willing of the human conscious cerebral cortex that banishes the troublesome lower willing of the subconscious midbrain and body functions of hunger, sex, and reproduction.

The conscious self, compensates for it having to often answer to the dominant less conscious and subconscious soul function, and its helplessness in the environment. It does so by ideating a first father god who can help alleviate internal struggle and provide for external care and protection. The conscious self of monotheistic word artists was troubled by what it saw as a curse of life, the subconscious functions of a mortal midbrain and body dynamic. In so doing, the word artists failed to perceive an animating soul and a sea of energy particles of the environment to be its true origin. Rather, the artist scribes opted for the spewing forth of spoken and written words about a monotheistic god.

The authors and redactors of the Genesis Garden of Eden story idolized a first father god, and by so doing disowned a real less conscious and subconscious animating internal soul that is a continuation of the nonconscious environment. The authors did so by creatively imagining and using a palate of words to artistically portray where the cultural group came from to be an external first father god. The imagined and artistic word portrait describing a willing first father is revered rather than a real internal animating and willing soul.

By so doing, the ideational image-making and word using conscious human self, claims supremacy over the wordless less conscious and subconscious animating and willing soul dynamic. While the less conscious and subconscious soul is partially amenable to guidance by the conscious self, it often disobeys and with wordless bodily urges forcefully demands that the self must obey and obtain what it wants to obtain.

Monotheistic word artists and a legion of adherents have failed to comprehend the origin of humans to be an internal less conscious and subconscious soul that is a continuation of the nonconscious environment. The conscious self of monotheistic word artists portrays a first father with words of story to identify human origin and to assume vicarious control. In the biblical Genesis story, the god conflicts with, curses, and banishes the first humans, alias the unrecognized soul.

The cerebral cortex of the brain asserts its dominance over the midbrain and body by creating a story that represents its presence to be a supreme first father god whose intelligent willing made the environment and life. This is the egocentric pride and glorification of the human cerebral cortex taking full credit for the origin of existence. This is a case of intelligence wrongfully and pridefully claiming supremacy and precedence over the less intelligent but true origin of life. The true origin of life is an internal animating and willing soul that is a continuation of energy particles of a supportive environment.

The Genesis story of a first father god cursing the first humans (3:14-19) really represents the cerebral cortex of the brain as it curses the midbrain and body dynamic of an animating and urging triune soul that functions as a hunger for food and water, sex and reproduction, and aggression. The story of a first father god versus the first humans is an artistic and mythic version of a real willing conflict between the higher conscious cerebral cortex and the lower less conscious and subconscious midbrain and body. The cerebral cortex represents its own existence via the ideational word and picture images of story to be an intelligent first father god, and represents the midbrain and body as the disobedient first humans of existence.

Through story images, the cerebral cortex asserts its dominance by having its figurehead, the god, make the first humans from the soil of the earth. The male cerebral cortex asserts its gender dominance by first making the male *adamah* or earthling, and then the female from the male body. The human body, portrayed as molded from a red soil, does have a real evolving origin from the chemistry and elements of the earth but no first father god exists as the animating mechanism. A first father who makes the first human is really an alias of the cerebral cortex of the brain that wants to have pseudo authority over what it cannot, the midbrain and body dynamic of an animating soul and the external environment.

The dynamic of an internal willing soul of hunger for food and water, sex and reproduction, and aggression, is a continuation of real metaphysical atom and electron energy particles of the environment.

With strong subconscious urges the midbrain and body willfully demand food and water, sex and reproduction, and aggression, and force the conscious cerebral cortex to acquire and will for what it wants to survive. In response, the Genesis monotheistic god, alias the cerebral cortex, willfully demands obedience from the first humans, alias the midbrain and body functions. This is the forever sin of separation of good and reason from bad and evil nonreasoning

The Garden of Eden story metaphorically describes the real dualistic willing functions of both, the cerebral cortex and the opposing yet complimentary primary functions of the midbrain and body. The authors utilized words images of artistic story to identify how order and disorder of an earthly life came to exist for humankind. The cerebral cortex artistically portrays its existence as a first father god who made order, and the midbrain and body are represented as the first humans who caused disorder for themselves and whose descendants continue to be disorderly to this day.

Monotheistic religions and their followers seek to remedy the disorder of existence by appealing to a first father to impose or restore order. A first father god story is a mythic means to subjectively restore or insure order for humans. Just like useless rituals such as baptism in water to wash away sins, monotheistic word art has no real effect in washing away or removing disorder or restoring ethical and physical order.

Slave

The mythic Garden of Eden was not a paradise made for the exclusive use of the first humans. The first two humans really served as serfs (Latin *servus*, slave) for the god who made it. They were to till and work the land of the first father's garden, and in exchange for guarding and protecting it, the god provided for the first humans "… every tree that is pleasant to the sight and good for food…." (Genesis 2:9)

"And Yahweh Elohim took the man, and put him into the garden of Eden to dress it and to keep it." (Genesis 2:15 King James Version)

"And Hashem Elohim took the adam and put him in the Gan Eden la'avod and to be shomer over it." (2:15 Orthodox Jewish Bible)

The Hebrew word *hashem* means name and is a substitute for the actual name of the god Yhwh, as it is not to be spoken or written. The adam or *adamah* means the red earthling, the first human made from the reddish blood-like mineral ochre of the earth. The word *la'vod*, means to till or work, while *shomer*, means to protect or guard.

Since the Garden was a paradise of all things made good, it has to be asked, guard or protect from what? The Garden of Eden was certainly not a paradise the way it has generally been accepted in later history. The Genesis first father made humans to work and care for the garden, to serve and obey him. This is a version of servitude and not able to escape from the god became a limitation. It was not long before the first humans soon found they had a free will and they did not have to always obey the first father in a servile manner. Endowed by the free will of their first father, the first humans began to disobey and soon obtained more of the god's knowledge for themselves.

Experiencing vulnerability in the environment, biblical word artists extricated themselves and their later followers from it by giving credence to the word portrait of a monotheistic god. In monotheistic religions, the exaggerated story character of a god represents the cerebral cortex of the brain, while the role of first father represents the reality of sexual reproduction by many biological forefathers. A first father character artistically and simply represents a shared family line of forefathers, and the combined strength of its members.

Human life is a continuation of the environment and as such is conditioned by it, and by a triune soul within the body that urges and hungers for food and water, wants to have sex and reproduce and to express aggression. Monotheistic writers sought to reduce the real slavish dependence of life on the external environment and its internal continuation as a triune soul. Monotheistic word artists ideated and wrote stories about a first father god who can moderate conditions of the environment and human behavior.

Witness to the spectacle of both dependence on conditions of the environment and struggling with the willing urges of life within, the conscious self of the cerebral cortex of the monotheistic brain subjectively responded by creatively imagining and sketching the word portrait story of a first father god.

Good Knowledge

The Genesis monotheistic god endowed the first humans with a free will not unlike his own good and evil capable will and of course they soon freely opposed him with it. To further complicate existence, the god separated off some of his good and evil knowledge and placed it where humans willfully and easily obtained it by ingesting a tree fruit. This scenario suggests there is an eternal duo, the opposing of willing and knowledge, and good and evil.

The existential angst of the Garden of Eden story, is that the free will endowed by the god, and the knowledge acquired from the first father's tree fruit were not all good as both also contained evil. (Genesis 3:5-6) Therefore, human free will and knowledge were contaminated forever more with both good and evil obtained from the first father. Humans have been doomed by their inherited free will and acquired knowledge and are cursed with an inability to remove and to replace both with an all good will and knowledge. The Genesis scenario represents a real limitation of the conscious cerebral cortex of the brain in opposition to the subconscious midbrain and body functions. Human willing is capable of both good and evil; the good willing of the conscious cerebral cortex, and evil willing urges of the less conscious and subconscious midbrain and body. This duality often perplexes conscious knowledge, so much so that the desperate artistic imagining and emotional clutching of a first father by many who are desperate, is accepted to be true and reliable knowledge.

A monotheistic god is only a subjective artistic word story and is not reliable objective knowledge. Circa 500 BCE, the knowledge of Middle East word artists was not sufficient to know that the origin of life is the environment, and that life is an evolving continuation of it.

Imagining a first father's strong will to be the fashioner of the environment, overlays the natural earth and is a subjective artistic way to control it. The imagining of a greater will that made the great environment and life, is a subjective way to vicariously control the willing-like changes of the earth and human willing. The idea of a super first father also reinforces human willing to be both good and strong enough to survive the competitive contest and various evils of life.

Sex

Artifact evidence suggests that circa 10,000 BCE it was known that acts of sexual intercourse caused pregnancy, birth, and the genealogical sequence of ancestors and descendants. It was not so apparent to know how the sequence of forefathers and mothers began. What occurred in the Middle East was a leap of creative artistic ideation and images written in story about a monotheistic god beginning of the environment and life. The first father made the first human in his own image (Genesis 1:26-27) and therefore endowed him with genitals like his own. The monotheistic god must have planned for humans to use their genitals as he endowed both male and female with the physiology for sexual reproduction. Therefore, it is ironic that the first father later cursed the humans for obtaining his own good and evil knowledge of sexuality from a good-tasting tree fruit.

In the biblical story, the first father is portrayed as "…walking in the garden in the cool of the day…." (Genesis 3:8) Not mentioned is whether the god was nude like his first humans who were both walking around naked and not ashamed, (Genesis 2:25) or if he wore clothing. That the first humans were nude in the presence of the bipedal first father, suggests he must have also been nude.

In the Garden of Eden story, the god's genitals are not mentioned and they play no active role in the making of human life. It is good that the first father god is modest and does not ever visibly reveal his nude form to humans.

Since the first human was made in the image of the god, if a sculpture or painting is to be made of the first father, unless clothed he would have to be represented as anatomically correct with a penis, testicles, and buttocks prominently displayed.

Somehow it was important for the first father to endow the first male human with a penis and testicles in the god's image, and later fashion the woman to have a vagina and womb. By endowing humans with genitals, it may be surmised that the god did have a plan for future human sexual reproduction. Certainly, the god did not give the first humans knowledge of what their genitals were for or how to use them. The first humans did not have clothes or cover themselves until just prior to expulsion from the Garden of Eden. (Genesis 3:21) Sometime prior to eating the fruit of good and evil, they must have wanted more knowledge about their bodies. The first father is surprised (Genesis 3:9-11) to find out that his first humans had curiosity and wanted to obtain more knowledge, even if it was half evil and included the use of genitals the god had made prior for sexual reproduction.

In the Garden story, the first woman is more to blame for her curiosity and suggests it was she who was most curious about knowledge, perhaps about her own body and genitals. Monotheistic religions ostensibly worship a first father but realistically worship a shared male and female biological origin of sexual reproduction. The monotheistic word art of a first father represents real biological reproduction of many forefathers and mothers. Monotheistic word artists subjectively ideated a first father who inexplicably made humans in his image with genitals, (Genesis 1:26-27) and then the god blamed humans for obtaining knowledge of how to use them and to sexually reproduce.

Circa 4 BCE, the monotheistic fatherly god with genitals impregnated a virgin girl by the name of Mary. Neither prior to or following this event, there have been no credible reports of the monotheistic god impregnating another woman. Mary had a son who grew up to be and to do only good, and although there are historical rumors about a sexual relationship between Jesus and Mary Magdalene, he is not reported as being intimate with a woman.

The portrayed first father god who is endowed with genitals, had a son who was undoubtedly endowed with genitals live a nonsexual life. The Christian message seems to be, what is good is to not have sex. Christian attention and the preoccupation to reduce the presence and influence of sex, and the absence of recreational sex in the lives of Mary and also Jesus, is a story way of reducing average individual willing for sex. Probably for good cause as sexual relationships are intense, usually troublesome, and promote all kinds of problems for individuals. Problems associated with sex and reproduction include having children, jealously, infidelity, divorce, child support, alimony, and domestic violence.

According to Catholic church doctrine, the hymen of Mary's vagina was not broken during impregnation and the birth of Jesus and she therefore remains "ever virgin." Christian story is the effort to remove the influence of troublesome urges of sexuality within humans, and instead to refine and promote its more acceptable expression of love. The Israelite Jesus directed individual willing to the love of a mutual shared origin and to one's fellow humans. (Mark 12: 28-34; Matthew 22: 36-40)

Poor Priests

Poor celibate Catholic priests, molesting the young through history all the while seeking refuge in the cerebral cortex of the brain that harbors the subjective idea of a monotheistic god. For priests, there is a psychological, legal, and monetary price to pay for preferring the subjective artistic idea of a monotheistic god over a real animating triune soul. The idea of a monotheistic god is impotent and many lose the struggle with the indwelling real power of the less conscious and subconscious triune soul as hunger for food, sex and reproduction, and aggression that overwhelms the subjective ideation of a first father.

Some individuals manage to tame the all-powerful triune soul but not many are able to do so. Only a few may reach a refuge of comprehension that the only real dimension where a monotheistic god resides is in the cerebral cortex neurons of the human brain.

Each person is their own problem of a rational conscious self and a less rational and irrational subconscious soul. This existential situation often becomes a problem not only for the person but also for others around them. Life really is a problem, easily observed in that humans are kept busy dealing with bodily demands of obtaining food and water, sex and reproduction, and with one's own aggression and the aggression of others. The various problems of life is why many gullible individuals seek to reduce or remove personal difficulties by accepting the priestly promoted great problem solver of a monotheistic god.

Sheepish

Ever since the dawn of monotheistic religions, the clever offer has been made to the unclever for the price of a donation or obedience, a first father god to save humans during life and death. The clever offer to the unwary is often made by a pastor, a Christian term defined as:

"A shepherd or herder, a caretaker of a flock of sheep who takes them to pasture and protects them from predators."

A pastor protects a sheep-like herd of humans from the troubles, dangers, and disasters of daily life with uplifting sermons, support, and counseling. The main offered pastoral protection is the spoken and written artistic word portrait of a monotheistic god. Humans are vulnerable and often helpless, and want to be taken care of by family members, friends, community, and government. There are many more foolish persons who want to be taken care of by a monotheistic god.

Monotheism is a first father cult, a false genealogy and an artistic work of spoken and written word art. Many individuals are encouraged to have faith and to depend on an ideational god within the cerebral cortex of their brain. Yet, the delusion or mistaken idea of a first father generates a false and dangerous sense of security by relying on what only exists subjectively. Humankind must eventually transcend its subjective reliance on the artistic theological knowledge and belief of a monotheistic god.

Not to do so exposes the lives of many trusting adherents of monotheism to objective risk and jeopardy.

To solve the beginning of existence with the story of a monotheistic god gave those artist scribes in possession of the word art portrait, a greater stature in the social group. Indeed, the word artists saw their role in life as representing the god of the culture. The monotheistic story of a first father is a spoken and written work of word art that subjectively elevates the origin of humans to a status that exceeds the all-powerful real environment. When looked at closely, at least some followers of monotheistic religions may be honest enough to admit that their life is shaped more by one real environment and not by a monotheistic god.

When questioned about the existence of a monotheistic god, some pastors have been observed to behave sheepishly, as if some small bit of conscience within must realize that a first father exists only subjectively and is a spoken and written work of word art. This is why when pressed or confronted about the existence of a god, a pastor may display a sheepish grin that suggests a secret embarrassment and shame in the presence of his followers who are often unwilling to voice their doubts.

A pastor may on occasion exhibit a sheepish grin when realizing on some level of awareness that he may look quite foolish to stubbornly insist on the objective existence of a first father god. The sheepish self-conscious mannerism suggests and reveals a monotheistic god to be subjective and therefore its existence does not require any objective evidence, only a foolish faith in the accepted idea.

The English title *reverend* means, one who is revered, referring to a Protestant church leader. A reverend is revered for encouraging humans to do what is good and to accept the word art portrait of a monotheistic god. The reverend promises that the god will save a person in life and also following death with a resurrection of body, spirit or breath, and free will. Unfortunately, this is a false hope, and the spoken words of a reverend about a first father furnish only subjective comfort to those in need.

While the accepted idea of a monotheistic god brings some individuals subjective relief, it is only the presence of an empathetic reverend and his kind and helpful words of advice that can bring to some real comfort to the life of an anxious individual.

The French word *cure* or *curate* is a title of a Catholic priest. The title is defined as a person who is tasked with the care and cure of souls. This is accomplished by directing attention away from a real soul that saves an individual by what it is, a continuation of a sea of energy particles of the environment that is resistant to destruction. Attention is instead wrongly directed to the word art portrait of a monotheistic god that only subjectively saves by reducing individual anxiety during the daily course of living and dying

God & Soul Theory and Jesus

Applying the propositions of the God & Soul Theory to the life of Jesus of Nazareth (circa 4 BCE-33 CE) furnishes an alternative hypothesis to the gospel versions of his life. The theory reveals a mostly natural or preternatural life of Jesus rather than the mythic supernatural stories of his existence. The monotheistic myth is, Jesus does not have original sin and is therefore not separate from the first father god. He is accepted by Christians to be and is portrayed as the offspring, the supernatural seed of a first father.

Theologians comment on Jesus that he was not willfully disobedient to the first father god like the first humans were and all humans have been thereafter. He did not use his free will to disobey, and unlike all other humans, did not separate himself from what is higher. Utilizing the propositions of the God & Soul Theory, it is more realistic to say of Jesus that his midbrain and body demands did not separate him from the higher functions of his cerebral cortex of the brain, alias the god.

To accomplish this feat, Jesus at least once, and perhaps at several other times, retreated to the desert to fast from food. (Mark 1:12-13; Matthew 4:1-11; Luke 4:1-13)

He is also portrayed in the gospels as abstaining from having sex, and he reduced aggression by expressing care and love. In this way Jesus arrived at the higher level of the cerebral cortex of the brain by getting free from the midbrain and body dynamic of the triune soul as a hunger for food and water, sex and reproduction, and aggression.

The gospel evidence suggests that Jesus must have attempted to bring about dominance of the conscious self, the cerebral cortex of the brain, and to reduce the subconscious urging forces of the midbrain and body functions, the dynamic of which is the triune soul. For the average individual, midbrain and body dominate in demands for food, sex and reproduction, and aggression. While the typical person spends much of daily life willing for these experiences, Jesus seems to have lived a life of moderation, observation, and experiential learning. Jesus was undoubtedly an innate genius in his family, or an old soul, or both, along with a genetic or developed extrasensory ability.

Guide to Good

The story of a monotheistic god is a simplistic folk guide to know the origin of the environment and life and provides a place to direct attention to where the good of protection and care can be obtained. The story god also furnishes commandments as a simple way to direct human behaviors to what is good and away from evil. For many people, a monotheistic god is a viable way out of the limiting and harmful situations of the environment. The first father serves as a parental authority to moderate interaction among humans, and functions as an externalized conscience for the internal demands of the midbrain and body dynamic of hunger for food, sex and reproduction, and aggression. Accepting the idea of an artistic word portrait of a monotheistic god furnishes a subjective escape from the limiting confines of the external environment and the internal animating soul.

The artist scribes of Genesis portray the written word portrait of a monotheistic god to function as a literary way to identify the origin of existence and to serve as an artistic not a realistic genealogy.

Unfortunately, western and southern European cultures slowly succumbed to the Middle East word artistry of a first father genealogy. Despite the growth of modern scientific knowledge, monotheistic religions continue to insist on spreading the contagion of a false first father genealogy as far and for as long as possible.

Clergy and rulers promote the artistic word portrait of a first father genealogy and use it to rule society. The surplus immature members of a susceptible population accept the artistic genealogy offered by monotheistic authority figures. The many foolish adherents then appeal to the first father god for care and protection during times of need in life and eventual death.

A monotheistic god story is an pragmatic artistic response to identify an unknown beginning of existence, and to furnish a directional guide for individual attention to what cares for humans. Attention is directed to a willing responsive first father and away from the willing-like unresponsive behaviors of the external environment and some fellow humans. A first father is an artistic response and pragmatic way to control individual behaviors by portraying the god dictating commands that serve to direct human behaviors toward good and away from the excessive force of evil.

The subjective idea of a strong willing monotheistic god adds pragmatic support for individual willing to survive life and death. A strong first father is needed as humans are helpless to save themselves from ageing and dying. When breathing ceases, the body dies and is soon cremated or buried to rot away until only bones remain, and with time they too disintegrate to dust. Change makes all things worthless and many people sense this to be so. Therefore, prone individuals accept the artistic word portrait of a monotheistic god offered by sacerdotalists as a way to subjectively survive life and death. Monotheistic oriented individuals reinforce their own willing to survive by inserting the subjective idea of a strong willing first father god into conscious attention when needed.

A monotheistic god is an imagined protector who has accompanied explorers and adventurers into unknown lands in search of wealth.

The god has helped to conquer and exploit heathens who have no knowledge of the first father. What the explorers of the past have unknowingly and knowingly encountered are what the subjective companion of a first father god is supposed to protect them from but did not.These are accidents, infectious diseases of viruses and bacteria, parasites, poisonous reptiles, dangers of weather and environment, aggression of indigenous peoples, and an often unfortunate and untimely death.

Poetic Musing

Once upon a time, many sighs of life became a question of how and why each must exist to live and then die? By and by, the response became a cry to the sky, to what is higher as a way to escape what is lower on the earth. The response was a lie by some artistic guy, who ideated and wrote down the word portrait of a first father as a way to give an added value of reason to life. The way to go in life for many people is to exert some willful effort and cling to the word portrait of a strong-willing monotheistic god. This is a long-accepted and subjective way to endure a good and evil existence.

Circa 500 BCE, artist scribes of Genesis affixed to the unknown origin of existence, the word portrait story of a monotheistic god. As a consequence, for many later adherents, the first father becomes a fixation with a repute of being a fixer of human problems. Not a first father god but the earth, the earth with its wide wide girth full of countless energy particles, gives birth to the many pleasures and pains of life and death.

Refuge

While some individuals willingly disobey their biological father, many more want to obey and do what pleases him. This psychological dynamic predisposes many people to accept the simple artistic word portrait of a monotheistic god, and to want to obtain approval from the first father. As portrayed in the book of Genesis, human free will can obey or disobey, act for or against, and this duality was provided to the first humans by a metaphorical monotheistic god.

To an ambivalent ability for willing the duality of good and evil, add knowledge acquired from the god's own tree, and there exists a compound problem of human life. Further, add the Genesis story that the first father made the human animating breath or spirit, free will, and body to be mortal and not long-lasting, and there is a triple problem traced to the monotheistic god.

The first father made a mess of existence, or more correctly the subjective idea of a monotheistic god is a messy idea that only childishly and poorly explains the origin of the environment and life. The first father god that oversees life and death is a subjective and comforting work of art, a word portrait that many people continue to accept and utilize to entice and proselytize others with. Monotheistic religions teach adherents to focus conscious attention to pray to a first father. Sacerdotalists do not teach followers to focus attention to better observe and to comprehend brain and body functions but instead to direct internal attention to an artistic word portrait that portrays an external origin of existence. For monotheistic religions, internal human willing is both good and evil and must be managed only by a greater external parental first father.

For young children who recognize some minor risks to their young lives, to be protected by a real family father is comforting. For childish adults who recognize many more serious threats to life, the subjective idea and assuring spoken and written word portrait of a super first father is even more comforting. Many otherwise normal adults continue to obtain assurance of care and protection by subjectively accepting the artistic word portrait of a first father god to be objective.

Mess

Life is a mess, composed of both order and disorder. Life becomes even more of a mess when the idea and word art story of a monotheistic god is mistaken by many people to be objective. A first father god is a subjective popular way to simplistically trace human genealogy back in time. Another huge mess consists of many ideas about the nonexistence or existence of a human soul.

Monotheistic religions deny there is a soul and only accept there will be a body resurrection by a super first father god. The existence of a soul is popular with many people who fervently hope they have one and that it will survive physical death. Among those who accept the existence of a soul, it is popularly assumed it is good and is worthy to be saved in some way.

Some individuals who have excess troubles and burdens of life, may prefer to destroy the physical body and hope to free the soul from life, or hold the view no soul exists to survive and rather choose the personal peace of oblivion. However, based on anecdotal reports and case studies of survival, oblivion will not occur following death. When humans die, the earth environment will not remember them. The gross materials of soil, water, and air will not remember an individual but the dimension of a sea of subtle energy particles of atom and electrons of which the environment is composed will remember. Particles of energy are omnipresent throughout the universe. Human life and its animating soul is a continuation of it, and will be remembered by an invisible dimension of an energy field.

Humans are a hot mess. They live and benefit from the good of a life-supporting earth, and are also challenged by evils or excessive forces of the environment from which many people die on a daily basis. Human body cells malfunction with disease, injury, genetic disorders, and age. The dynamic conscious self of the cerebral cortex of the brain is a mess, with attention often distracted by sensations, and undisciplined and uncontrolled sequences of picture images of now, past, and future. The less conscious and subconscious animating soul is a dynamic mess of varying urging efforts to survive as triune willing urges of hunger for food and water, sex and reproduction, and aggression.

A monotheistic god is a subjective way to put the best spin on life, and to ameliorate the messiness of living. In the biblical Genesis story, a first father god is portrayed as the character who made humans to exist, and is said to care about them, and yet ever refrains from cleaning up the mess of life.

Therefore, it is up to humans who must be responsible and through the use of observation, trial and error learning, and testing of science, to clean up the mess of life as much as is possible. Unfortunately, life will always be somewhat messy. Trial and error and heuristic learning is the only real way to clean up some of the messes of human life. The God & Soul Theory contributes to the cleaning up of the subjective mess of a monotheistic god, and also clarifies the murky messiness of a human soul by better defining it to be a real dynamic that is resistant to destruction.

Zoroastrianism

Circa 1200 BCE in the country of Persia, today known as Iran, an Aryan prophet by the name of Zoroaster, founded the religion of Zoroastrianism. Tradition says the prophet had a vision while gazing into a fire, and declared thirty-two hundred years ago that both good and evil are eternal twins.

"In the beginning there were primal twins, spontaneously active, these are the Good and the Evil…." (Yasna 30:3)

Zoroaster's revelation was of supernatural twin figures having intentions, and eventually were given the names of Ahura Mazada, the origin of good, light and truth, and Ahriman, origin of evil, darkness, and lies. Zoroaster's teachings became the religion known today as Zoroastrianism, and a follower of the teachings then had the personal choice to will good thoughts, words, and deeds, or evil thoughts, words and deeds.

The personalities of Ahura Mazda and Ahriman came into existence simultaneously and are therefore not identical but are fraternal twins. The twins are equal, and this anthropomorphic metaphor explains the existence and the back and forth struggle between good and evil in the environment and within humans. This way of thinking, of good versus evil, has been shown by scholars of history to be the influential basis for the later monotheistic religions of Judaism, Christianity, and Islam.

Historically influenced by Zoroastrianism, Judaism is a religion that portrays life to be a conflict between both good and evil willing and knowledge. Word artist scribes of Judaism saw fit to change the earlier Zoroastrianism scenario from fraternal twin conflict to a paternal conflict of a first father god with his willfully disobedient first humans. The religion of Zoroastrianism is based on the model of family conflict between twin siblings, one good and the other evil. In Judaism, the dual sibling conflict scenario of Zoroastrianism was replaced by a parent-offspring model. Genesis fraternal conflict was only retained in the lesser biblical story of Cain and Abel as told in Genesis 4.

In chapter 1 of Genesis, the monotheistic god made all things good. The first father then endowed humans with a good and evil capable free will similar to his own. Using their free will capable of the good of obedience or the evil of disobedience, the first humans willingly brought the sin of separation, struggle, and suffering on themselves by acquiring the god's own good and evil knowledge from the fruit of his special tree. The god then cursed the humans and the ground of the earth (Genesis 3:17) which brought forth evils including "thorns and thistles." (Genesis 3:18) Unlike good and evil coming from either of the Zoroastrianism twins, all things good and evil are traced to a monotheistic god.

The metaphorical Zoroastrianism twins represent the good and evil things in the environment, such as geological events, weather, and animals. Within humans, the good twin represents the cerebral cortex of the brain, alias the conscious self. The evil twin represents the midbrain and body, alias the dynamic less conscious and subconscious soul. Both are co-rulers. This is what the noble Zoroaster saw in his vision, the twin good and evil existing in the environment, and as a continuation of the earth the twin rulers represent what is innate within humans as dynamic psychological and physiological internal functions of brain and body behaviors.

Alma Mater

To attend a university or college is to have an *alma mater*. The word *alma* is Latin variously meaning, "nourishing, nursing, fostering, and kind." The adjective was used by the Romans to refer to their goddesses such as Ceres, goddess of grains and agriculture, and Cybele the earth mother or mountain goddess. *Mater* is the Latin word for mother. An *alumnus* is a university graduate who has been nursed and nourished by knowledge obtained from his alma mater, his kind foster mother. In the Latin-based languages of Italian and Spanish, *alma* also refers to what animates human life, and translates into English as either spirit or soul.

During early medieval times in Europe, monasteries were built by and for monks as a refuge from often barbaric behaviors of fellow humans. The monastic building complex included a *scriptorium*, a place to copy and store manuscripts. The building complex eventually developed into universities of learning replete with libraries. The rise of European universities began with the university of Bolonga in Italy circa 1088 CE and in England the university of Oxford circa 1196. The universities of Paris and Cambridge followed during the 1200s, and by 1500 CE there existed more than eighty in western Europe.

While only males were instructors, the rise of universities suggests a move away from the monastic emphasis on a first father god of theology who cursed the first humans (Genesis 3:16-19) for obtaining more knowledge, to a more benign maternal patience and acceptance of learning. Biological birth, life, and nourishment comes from the mother, as does much of early childhood knowledge originate from interaction with her. In a printed artwork of the emblem of Cambridge University in London, dating to circa 1600, a woman is portrayed nude from the waist up, and the rest of her body is concealed by a pedestal with the words, *Alma Mater Canta Brigia*. The female figure is portrayed with milk flowing from her breasts and in her right hand she holds beams of the sun and in her left hand a goblet, above which is a small cloud raining into it. There is an olive wreath around her head and a small crown of a mural of buildings of the university. There are two trees growing on each side of her image. In the universities, an expansion of knowledge occurred beyond the narrow confines of theology, the knowledge of a monotheistic male god.

Following biological birth, a second kind of birth and growth is an increase of education and obtaining of knowledge. A university education was equated to a new birth and new life of nourishing knowledge. When an individual conscious self obtains the extra nourishment of education, it furnishes many more options for the cerebral cortex of the brain, and reduces the influence of the subconscious midbrain and body dynamic of the soul. By attending a university, an individual learns and lessens the influence of the midbrain and body dynamic of a less conscious and subconscious triune soul of hunger for food, sex and reproduction, and aggression. Education must have contributed to the lessening of barbaric behaviors during the time, and may have contributed to the origin and use of the word gentleman.

Interestingly, there is no fatherly institution of higher learning known as an *"alma pater."* The *alma mater* or kind mother suggests a change of emphasis away from a monastic focus on the theology of a monotheistic god. In the universities there was added liberal arts courses such as arithmetic, geometry, astronomy, logic, grammar, and rhetoric, all taught in Latin. With a maternal orientation, there was a liberal tendency to expand to other areas of learning, and of course a few hundred years later this has resulted in the modern emphasis on observation and testing of the modern sciences.

Bright Spot

Humans often experience a poignant lack of control of the external willing-like changes of the environment as repetitive cycles of day and night, seasons, and weather; these events occur without regard to humans or their activities. There are out of control human experiences of microorganisms and parasites that willfully infect and cause disease and medical conditions. Life is vulnerable to the willing of poisonous and predatory animals, and the willing aggression of family members, friends, and enemies.

Humans also experience the difficult to control internal conscious and subconscious willing functions of their midbrain and body.

The potential for harm, helplessness, and hopelessness though minimized by intelligent caution, lingers and cannot ever be completely excluded from human experience. Individuals ever struggle to counteract their poignant existential angst.

Circa 500 BCE in the Middle East, the willing effort to comprehend existence with all of the possible and oftentimes difficult to control experiences, resulted in an artistic response to lighten the burdens of life. Biblical word artists subjectively ideated a first father in the cerebral cortex of their brain, and writing in the word portrait story of Genesis, elevated it to the status of a god to brighten the dark days and nights of life and death.

Life is not to see who can successfully go from pleasure to pleasure and to have the most fun, it is about who can look ahead and to prudently avoid the many pain spots of life. Life is spotty, it consists of small spots of pleasures interspersed with small and many large spots of pain, suffering, depression and despair. A monotheistic god is for many people a subjective bright spot, a way to brighten an often real dim and dismal earthly existence.

Not completely satisfied with real natural bright spots of the physical supportive earth, sun, moon, and stars that consist of metaphysical particles of energy, monotheistic artist scribes imagined and wrote a word portrait story of a metaphorical monotheistic god. For many people, the subjective bright spot of a first father god outshines a real palpable objective environment.

The bright spot of a monotheistic god shines only subjectively in the cerebral cortex of the human brain and nowhere else and is a way to dispel the doom and gloom of life. The bright spot of a monotheistic god has been made by humans to cast some light, to illuminate the origin of existence, and to lighten the minor and major dark spots of life and death. A first father of all later fathers is a genealogical bright spot kindled by a passionate need to know and to portray the beginning, to shed some light on and to reveal the unknown origin of existence.

The artistic ideated story of a strong willing first father god is a subjective bright spot on which to focus attention and in so doing to lighten and fortify human willing.

Fortification

The word fortify is defined as:

"To strengthen and secure with fortifications, to encourage and reinforce emotionally, mentally, and physically; to add alcohol, vitamins, or minerals to food so as to make it more tasty or nutritious."

A monotheistic god subjectively fortifies an individual, emotionally, mentally, and physically. By swallowing the word story of a first father and adding it to one's collections of ideas about existence, like alcohol, it both stimulates and relaxes a person to feel better about life. Like food, the idea of a monotheistic god nourishes a person and provides emotional and mental strength to continue to live despite difficult times.

Knowing the origin story of existence, is a way of fortifying an individual from uncertainty and anxiety of an unknown beginning. A first father god is a subjective way of reinforcing individual and cultural identity, and of fortifying against the environment, other life forms, and harmful humans. A monotheistic god is a metaphorical fort, defined as:

"A fortified enclosure, building, or position able to be defended against an enemy."

A monotheistic god is a mental construction, a place of refuge and safety, a subjective enclosure, an artistic word-built fort constructed by monotheistic word artist scribes and dished out by sacerdotalists for public consumption. Taking refuge in the subjectively constructed fortification of a monotheistic god is comforting, reduces risks, and offers protection during the battles and struggles of life.

The enemy to be defended against is the environment, other life forms, harmful fellow humans, chance, and time. A monotheistic first father presented in a word portrait of story is a subjective fortification, a way to encourage, strengthen, reinforce and fortify an individual emotionally, mentally, and physically.

Help

Rather than observe and search the environment for the origin of life, early genealogical oriented biblical word artists searched their own subjective ability of the cerebral cortex of the brain to ideate or imagine, and wrote a story about a monotheistic god and the Genesis of existence. The biblical story of a monotheistic god is a subjective help to identify the origin of existence, and a place where help can be obtained. To say there is no first father god is to say there is no help and that the individual is alone in the environment and among other humans. When no help is available from fellow humans, then an individual may convert to a monotheistic religion and accept the subjective artistic word portrait of a first father god. A monotheistic god is an orientation away from potential dangers and painful situations, not to nothing but to something that can help. Retreating from real experience to a subjective ideated willing of a monotheistic god that has willed all of existence, helps to support individual willing to persevere during life and death.

Human willing for food, sex and reproduction, and aggression often leads to the helpless situations of life. Monotheistic religions trace the beginning of human willing to a first father god as a subjective way to solve the problems of life but the maneuver more often leads to a false sense of security and blindly taking risks that endanger and complicate real-life situations. Since a monotheistic god is subjective and artistic and not realistic, it can never solve the real problems of human willing and the good and evil experiences of existence.

A willing monotheistic god is an artistic way to help explain the origin of existence, serves to encourage confidence and to persevere through the willing-like changes of the environment, and functions to direct and command humans to will more of good and less evil behaviors.

A first father is given credit for helping to moderate the environment, to intervene in life and death situations, and will someday even resurrect numerous long dead bodies.

First Father Willing

A monotheistic god is a symptom of an excess of subjective ignorance and a lack of objective knowledge. Human willing to survive is externalized and artistically imagined to be a first father whose willing made all existence. The imaginal strong willing of a monotheistic god compensates for the weak vulnerable willing of many humans.

The monotheistic religions utilize spoken and written words of story to explain the origin of existence. A monotheistic god represents the greater willing-like change of the environment and the energy particles of which it consists. The first father god also represents the shared group willing of sexual reproduction. A monotheistic god is a tool utilized by human authority figures to insist they are approved of by the first father and are sanctioned to rule. A monotheistic willing god encourages the mutual good willing of members of a social group and is a role model used by parents to train children as a way to get them to will what is good.

The subjective idea of a strong willing monotheistic god provides a model for a good attitude and is a pragmatic saving optimism from the pessimistic, depressing, and harmful experiences of human life. Having reached the limit of individual knowledge and effective willing, the idea of a first father provides many people the fortitude and strength to continue to learn and live. Subjectively accompanied by the idea of a first father, it is possible to maintain a higher attitude of courage and to endure life during situations of danger and harm.

Rational

The biblical Genesis story of an intelligent monotheistic god is an artistic attempt to rationalize life, to convince the listener or reader that life has been rationally intended, made, and is supervised.

The mistaken and irrational idea of a rational first father god is a way of rationalizing existence by the marginally rational cerebral cortex of the human brain. The spoken and written word portrait of a monotheistic god is an artistic way some humans subjectively imagine and reach out to what is more rational. A first father is a way to direct attention away from and reduce irrational experiences of living. Just as a monotheistic god is reasonable and rational, so should humans also be but this is not the case at all.

Human ability for reasoning is a function of the cerebral cortex of the brain, also known as the conscious self. The human midbrain and body dynamic of an animating soul is not rational in its willful triune urges for food, sex and aggression. A rational god is a way monotheistic religions distance themselves from a sensed but non-recognized irrational triune soul of subconscious forceful urges. The internal animating irrational soul is ignored by biblical word artists for a rational external father ancestor and animator.

Barely rational and mostly irrational, in the biblical Genesis story human life is traced back in time through a false genealogical origin story of forefathers to a greater rational intelligence of a first father god. In this way, biblically oriented humans artistically imagine and subjectively save themselves from irrational experiences of life and death. An artistic word portrait of a rational first father who dictates commands, reinforces rational human behaviors. An ideated rational god is a subjective tool to rationalize and shape human life experience to be more rational. A portrayed intelligent ruling god of the greater environment is an artistic way to inspire some humans to learn and to increase their own reason and knowledge.

A monotheistic god story is accorded some validity only by having a foundation for it based on real fatherly experiences. The promoted word portrait of a first father relies on and is layered upon and supported by fond memories of real fathers and grandfathers. For monotheistic religions, the artistic word art story of a great first father represents a connection with the greater number of genealogical forefathers (Genesis 5) and their collective sexual reproduction.

The supposed will of a single first father represents the willing group behavior of male sexual reproduction and aggression to survive.

Story

It is necessary to comprehend where a monotheistic god comes from. The vaunted Genesis story of the beginning of existence in chapter 1, really began in the cerebral cortex of a human brain by a word artist author. The cerebral cortex of the monotheistic brain, represents where life has come from by ideationally identifying it to be a first father god and portraying it in the word art of story. Therefore, monotheistic religions must be correctly subsumed under the category of art history. The genealogical first father of monotheism is artistic not realistic, and is metaphorical not metaphysical. A genealogy traced to a monotheistic god is subjective word art and is therefore a mere representation of a long line of many real but unknown forefathers.

In the Garden of Eden story, a dynamic soul is ignored for an idolized first father. This is the sin of monotheism, humans separating themselves from their origin by accepting the subjective artistic word portrait of a first father god to be objective. Monotheistic religions prefer a first father god animator, and for them an animating human soul as a continuation of the environment does not exist. The monotheistic myth of a first father god whose willing is immortal, is a metaphor for a human soul, a triune of willing urges for food and water, sex and reproduction, and aggression that is resistant destruction.

Life does not come from the subjective artwork of words about a monotheistic god. Life grows from an inner animating and willing triune soul that is a continuation of a seeming lifeless environment but which is really a ground, a seething sea of energy particles that animate life. For those unable to know much about energy particles that really exist, better to continue along with the primitive nonrealistic tradition of monotheistic ideation and word story of a first father god.

Special

Circa 500 BCE, early Middle East monotheists observed that humans are prone to chance, aggression, ageing, and death just like members of all species. Imagining a special monotheistic god that began existence, translates as a way of seeing human existence as special and not like any other species of life. By looking to the past and a monotheistic god, humans can better survive and thrive. A first father is artistic not realistic and is a way of feeling subjectively protected during life and death experiences. A monotheistic god is a subjective approximation, a word defined as:

"An inexact and limited accuracy for a given purpose or need."

To identify an unknown origin, monotheistic religions prejudicially approximate it to a human-like beginning of a first father who is then further exaggerated and idolized to be a god who can provide care and protection. What a person values as special or unique, produces a feeling of pleasure and upliftment. Circa 2500 years ago, biblical word artist scribes identified the unknown origin of existence to be a monotheistic god which must have brought them a feeling of creative pleasure. Yet, a first father god furnishes only subjective upliftment and can never provide realistic intervention.

When life was observed to end and the body ceased to breathe and move, biblical word artists reacted by ideating a monotheistic god who could render some external assistance to helpless humans. The ceasing of life in the body can be painful for the dying and for those who witness the sudden or slow process. What or who to appeal to? Forefathers cannot be expected to prevent pain, death, and decay, or to help humans. Only a super strong and knowledgeable grand first father who made the environment and all of life is imagined to save humans from the dangers of life and eventual death by resurrecting the body.

When life no longer exists within the body and breathing ceases, nothing can be observed to survive physical death.

Further convincing evidence of nothing worthwhile existing in the body, is that it soon begins to decay. Genesis word artist writers ignored what animates humans inside and imagine it to exist only outside of the body. Humans who accept monotheistic religions separate themselves from what animates life when they imagine it to exist exclusively outside of the body as a special first father god. The deluding of humans by teaching them that the subjective word art of a first father god is objective and true, is a cruel and unforgivable sin of separation from a real environment.

Great

The religions of Judaism, Christianity, and Islam, trace their ethnic origin to an ideated first father who is artistically exaggerated and idolized to the status of a god. The existence of a monotheistic god is a way of making a person or a culture feel greater and better about existence. Having a great ancestor contributes to individual and cultural greatness. Not having a great ancestor, existence will not be so great.

Lacking a monotheistic god, many people will feel abandoned on earth and will find life minimally tolerable, and quite a few will not be able to tolerate it at all. To strengthen vulnerable human willing, or to moderate the excess force of human willing known as evil, the task is accomplished by subjectively recognizing the stronger willing of a first father who will reward or punish. The artistic word art portrait of a monotheistic god only subjectively rewards an individual and not objectively.

The word art portrait of a monotheistic god is a faulty way of enlarging, of making the conscious willing of the human cerebral cortex to be greater than the willing-like change of the environment. The cerebral cortex of the brain glorifies a super willing that made and must therefore manage an often-unmanageable existence. While convincing to many people, this artistic subjective maneuver impairs clear psychological comprehension. The cerebral cortex of monotheistic adherents is enlarged and ballooned in size and importance by the inflating egoistic idea of a first father ancestor god.

Yet, in terms of volume of brain neurons, based on modern neuroscience best estimate, the conscious cerebral cortex contains only sixteen billion neurons while the subconscious midbrain contains seventy billion of them. Looks convincingly like the greater willing is not to be found with the cerebral cortex (and central nervous system) and its ideated first father god but with the midbrain and body (autonomic nervous system). The dynamic and dominant triune less conscious and subconscious soul pulls individual attention of the conscious self to what it wants, and pushes the cerebral cortex for conscious behaviors to acquire food and water, sex and reproduction, and aggression.

Attention to an unlimited first father temporarily removes attention from human limitations in the environment and an inner limiting ability for effective willing and knowing. Sacerdotalists tell potential converts to direct attention to and accept the word portrait of a first father god and in so doing they will experience the subjective relief of belief. A subjective delusion but for many people a pragmatic one.

A capable person must reward themselves with the comprehension that a monotheistic god is a verbal and written work of word art. An insightful person must also reward their own comprehension with observation and knowledge of the triune soul to be a dynamic of hunger for food and water, sex and reproduction, and aggression. Better to develop the recognition and comprehension of a real animating soul that is a continuation of a great sea of energy particles, and a continuation of a greater inexhaustible cosmological motion without beginning or ending. Ergo, humans have a real triune soul that as a continuation of energy particles of the environment is resistant to destruction.

Worth

Some things are wanted but never obtained, while for all things gotten, unceasing change makes them less than worthwhile. Boredom soon sets in and experience becomes jaded. What is new eventually wears out, becomes old and worn.

All things eventually become worthless and fit to be discarded, left behind, and eventually forgotten.

A first father god exists only in a word portrait story that has subjective worth but no real objective value at all. For monotheistic religions, nothing worthwhile is considered to exist within the dead and decaying human body. Based on these dual conceived errors of a monotheistic god and the nonexistence of a soul, many people are fearful of oblivion and readily accept on faith, belief, and tradition that a first father exists who will remember to resurrect their worthy spirit or breath, free will, and body.

A feeling of individual worthlessness comes from observing the fragility and vulnerability of human life. Seeking to improve or strengthen humankind with a long-lasting and stronger willing to better survive, word artist scribes and later sacerdotalists direct the attention of humankind to the spoken and written word portrait of a monotheistic god. The real willing that is greater than conscious human willing, is the less conscious and subconscious willing of a triune soul within the body. The willing soul is a continuation of the greater willing-like change of the environment, in turn a continuation of a greater cosmological force that exists on its own to ever move the universe.

Separation

From the supportive environment life evolved to exist separate from but dependent on the earth, sun, and moon. Evolution separated to function differently but complimentarily, various organs of the human body. The conscious cerebral cortex of the brain and central nervous system processes, function differently from the less conscious and subconscious autonomic nervous system of midbrain and body functions. The conscious cerebral cortex of the brain evolved an ability to transform sensations into picture images of objects portrayed in a space and time sequence. In the cerebral cortex of the brain evolved separate conscious willing from subconscious willing functions of midbrain and body.

Meanwhile, circa 500 BCE in the Middle East, there occurred an artistic separation that directed human attention away from observation of the environment and brain and body functions, to a first monotheistic god story. Rather than directing attention to observe, biblical word artists subjectively focused attention to ideate the story of a monotheistic god. Prayer or talking to a first father is a delusion, a mistaken idea, as it accepts attention to be directed to an objective god when it is really a subjective focus on an artistic word portrait of story.

While requiring more curiosity and effort, individual attention must be directed and trained to observe less conscious and subconscious willing functions of body cells and organs that are a continuation of the environment. Exploring and observing the dynamics of the conscious self and the less conscious and subconscious soul, true and reliable knowledge can be obtained about the human condition. Monotheism is a superficial shortcut of faith and belief that requires little effort and is simple ideation. Observation and learning require more effort and time to explore the brain and body dynamics of a conscious self and subconscious soul.

Good and Bad News

Now for the news, which is both good and bad. Unfortunately, good and bad news has always existed and will remain so daily for the foreseeable future. The good news is, there is a first father god. A monotheistic god serves to identify the origin of the environment and life, and is reputed to provide care and protection to those who ask. The god renders subjective help and hope to many people who are helpless and hopeless.

The bad news is, a monotheistic god exists only subjectively and not objectively. By imagining and writing a word portrait of a first father god, the cerebral cortex of the brain finds a subjective way to direct and control the nonresponsive environment and human behaviors. A monotheistic god is half real as it does exist as a subjective idea in the cerebral cortex but does not exist objectively outside of the brain.

The God & Soul Theory asserts this is a realistic view of partial atheism. The first father god of monotheistic religions is a prescientific and artistic way of identifying where the environment and life comes from. A monotheistic god is derived not from reasoning, mathematics, or science but from subjective artistic ability by ideating a word art story as a pragmatic way to make known an unknown beginning of the environment and life. Through the word art of story, a monotheistic god is a way of providing subjective but not real and objective care and protection to those in dire need. Claiming the word art story of a monotheistic god to be objective is how some humans obtain a sanction to rule over those who are susceptible to parental feelings of dependence. A monotheistic god is a convincing idea to many humans, and yet, the wide acceptance of a first father furnishes no guarantee that it is real and true.

The second good news is found in the writings of Indo-European cultures that have always insisted humans do have a real animating soul. This is good news for many people, and probably bad and the worst possible news for a few. For an observant few, the soul is a continuation of the energy particles of the environment and is therefore resistant to destruction and can repeat many times through many lives. Surrounded by unmistakable evidence of repetition such as cycles of day and night, moon phases, cyclical change of the seasons, how is it possible that an individual could possibly consider that life is not related to them. Humans are not free of these immense cosmic cycles and indeed are a continuation of them.

What blots out a real cosmological connection is the subjective artistic attempt to reduce and gain more freedom from inexorable cosmic cycles of the universe by utilizing the word portrait story of a monotheistic god. A first father is a subjective artistic effort to reduce human bondage poignantly felt to be at the mercy of the environment. Humankind strives to be free by subjectively imagining a monotheistic god that made and can control the environment and life. Since a first father made the environment, then the all-powerful god can alter the functions of the environment such as weather, volcanoes, and earthquakes that oppress human existence.

Yet, the liberating knowledge of a first father god occurs only as a subjective ideation in the cerebral cortex of the brain and is portrayed only in a superficial word art portrait of story.

The good news existence of a soul does not come from monotheistic religions. Monotheistic theology insists that humans have a breath or spirit, a free will, and a body, all three of which are mortal and must be reanimated and resurrected by an external first father god. Monotheists prefer not to die and want to continue to live, preferably in the same body. For monotheistic religions, no surviving animating soul exists within the human body. Monotheistic religions all agree that animation of the body is completely dependent on what is outside of it, a first father god. For science, what animates the living body is completely outside of it as the supportive environment. The biological functions of the human body are imbued with and are a continuation of the conditions, rhythms, and behavior habit patterns of the environment.

Both monotheistic religions and the sciences fail to fully recognize what animates the body inside. Science ignores the evidence of many anecdotal accounts and case studies that suggest that the human soul consisting of habit patterns, may continue to coherently survive outside of the body and can recur to live again. Perhaps someday in the not too distant future, science may announce news of recognizing and accepting the existence of an animating human soul, and that as a continuation of a sea of energy particles will conclude that it is also resistant to destruction.

Front Man

Traditionally, when humans need a way to control social behaviors, they may agree to elect a leader who sets up the authority of a government and that in turn may devise a legal system to supervise and to enforce rules and laws. As has occurred in the past, some artistic individuals may creatively imagine, and many will accept, the spoken and written word art portrait of a monotheistic god to be in charge of humankind.

The Old Testament or Tanak employs the artistic literary character of a first father to dictate commandments and direct individual willing into acceptable group behaviors. Artistically imagining a monotheistic god, a super first father, is a way of directing individuals and cultural groups and making existence subjectively safer than it would ordinarily be. A god character of story is a literary device to designate the origin of existence and to supervise human behaviors. A monotheistic god is in a sense a front man, a term defined as:

"A nominal leader of a group or organization who lacks real power or authority; a person used as a cover to lend respectability to some nefarious or questionable activity."

A monotheistic god is a nominal character in a word art story of where the environment and life come from. The written word portrait of a first father god is spoken of and commonly accepted as a way to make known human origin. Only in story does the nominal god vocally dictate commandments in his position as the maker and first father leader of monotheistic cultures.

Existing only as a nominal word portrait, the god lacks an objective existence and has no power, only a subjective authority in the lives of those who accept it. The god adds some respectability to human origin, and the questionable activities of life, consisting as it does of many evils and nefarious behaviors. Attention directed to a monotheistic god is a nefarious activity that covers over the real origin of life, an internal triune soul that is a continuation of a sensed but unseen sea of energy particles of the environment.

A first father god is nominal, exists only subjectively in name and word portrait stories. If an all good monotheistic god does exist, then humans would be all good rather than both good and evil. The good and evil willing of humans is a direct continuation of the good and evil willing and knowing of a metaphorical Genesis first father. A good monotheistic god made humans with a breath or spirit, a free will, and a body but without a soul and so he must then inconveniently resurrect the physical body.

Maybe, just maybe, the Middle East god exhibits a schmear of metaphysical incompetence by not having working knowledge of a soul.

A good god is a monotheistic subjective idea that exists only as a spoken and written artistic word portrait. The Middle East and its monotheistic religions are a geographic culture that ignores the existence of a soul, to foolishly hope for a body resurrection. Further east on the continent of Asia, the Hindu culture of India correctly focused attention on and investigated the human soul or *atma* and mistakenly misidentified it to be blissful and good. Western culture accepts the existence of a monotheistic god and conflates it with the popular notion of a soul that is good and worthy of saving. A monotheistic god paired with the folk tale of a good soul, are both extremely popular western delusions about existence.

First Father

To accept the existence of a monotheistic god makes it easier for many people to get through the difficulties of life and an impending death. A first father god story is a cobbled together artistic version of how the environment and life have come to exist. Looked at and examined closely, it is obvious that monotheistic scriptures are written artistic word art. Yet, only a few take the time to look more closely, just as most do not notice the finer details of a painting and are only concerned with the overall aesthetic impression and appearance of the artwork.

Accepting the objective existence of a familial first father is a subjective way of identifying an unknown origin, and is a way to find and obtain support and stability in an often fragile and unstable life. The existence of a monotheistic god is a subjective way of forming a simple ideation switch that can easily be turned on by an adherent when an artificial light is needed during the dark experiences of life. The easily turned on ideational switch of a first father god lightens daily burdens and brightens the day of many a downhearted individual.

Worshiping a word art portrait of a shared first father god is a way of saying the members of a culture are all family members. Yet, the artistic word portrait must be put away to see with clarity that all of life shares and is a continuation of a single cosmological sea of energy particles of the environment. To ignore an internal soul as do monotheistic religions, and to further ignore life to be a continuation of the external environment, and to instead accept the word portrait of a monotheistic god, is a necessary delusion for an excessive number of the earthly population.

The artistic ideation of a good god is a subjective nostrum in response to the various maladies of life. Adherents of monotheistic religions are patients who present with an ideational infection, an acquired ailment of grandiose super egoism. The dictates of a monotheistic god are but the dictations of word artist scribes. Jewish word artists surveyed the previous generations of many forefathers and inflated the numbers to artistically ideate a first father ancestor. The scribes then further exaggerated the size of a first father to the extra-large importance of a greater god. The resulting word story was their way to artistically enlarge their own ability to know the origin of existence.

Experiencing helplessness in the environment, and also in resisting the urging soul within as the dynamic of hunger for food and water, sex and reproduction, and aggression, is too excruciating for most. The artistic word story imagery of a monotheistic god forms a simple word shelter, and the relief of belief provides subjective assistance for a shaky existence.

The written word portrait of a monotheistic god is an artistic and mendacious explanation of where the environment and life come from. The deception was begun by biblical word artist scribes circa 500 BCE, and was later accepted and perpetuated by many individuals, and tolerated by Middle East and western cultures. The storybook guidance of a monotheistic tradition misguides many people, leading them astray by directing attention to an artistic ideated and subjectively written word portrait of a monotheistic first father god.

Ruler

To bring order to a bunch of troublemaking egos of a human population, there must be a bigger and stronger ego to take charge. If a real human leader does not step up to the challenge, then in Middle East cultures, word artist scribes wrote stories about the strong ego of a monotheistic god who made the environment and life, and to whom all smaller human egos must submit.

By knowing the origin of existence, the word artist scribes of monotheistic religions elevated themselves with the story of a god who made all things. The artists who possessed copies of the word art portrait of a monotheistic god, had special knowledge of the highest authority and thereby used it to rule the culture. Those with copies of the word story document elevated themselves to rule over the culture, or to co-rule by supporting political and military authority needed for protection. Rulers of the past and continuing today are all too often assassinated by rivals, a disgruntled mob, or a majority population of a culture during a revolution or civil war.

Monotheistic artist writers produced a work of word art about a powerful first father ruler who in the past made the environment and life. In this way, monotheistic authorities who have knowledge of the first father can rule for him and thereby deflect aggression directed toward them from the ruled, to the ruling protective god who sanctions the rulers. Wily rulers often announce publicly that their rule is associated with or approved and protected by a monotheistic god; a shrewd and safe political move. Throughout history, those who have claimed to possess knowledge of an unknown beginning of existence, could then rule for the absentee all-powerful ruling monotheistic god.

The rulers of many cultures have always been those who set up a government bureaucracy of laws and military, and those who rule for the unseen gods behind the scene who made events like storms, rain, and drought to happen. There were human rulers and those humans who had knowledge of unseen god rulers, always portrayed artistically with visual images or verbal and written words.

Metaphorical

Circa 500 BCE in the Middle East cultures of Judah and Israel, it was announced by scribal word artists that they had an answer to where the environment and life come from. In an effort to know the beginning of existence, it was artistically written in a book by word art scribes that "In the beginning..." (Genesis 1:1), later calculated to be circa 3081 BCE, a monotheistic first father made all things.

A monotheistic god is not metaphysical but is metaphorical and can only be traced and observed to exist in the knowing of the cerebral cortex of the human brain. A first father god is metaphorical not metaphysical, and that is why only subjective faith or belief is needed and not objective proof. Humans display the existence of what is higher when they accept the idea of a first father god in their cerebral cortex of the brain. In interaction with others, a person who accepts a monotheistic god does so by demonstrating a higher familial and polite attitude toward others and generally avoids coarse behaviors, or at least attempts to do so.

Metaphysical

There are physical and metaphysical problems of life. The majority of humans have eyes only for what is physical. Most experience and know of physical problems of body and brain and the environment. Less known is the answer to the metaphysical problem and question of what animates life and what if anything survives death. A monotheistic god is a problem as many confuse the subjective idea of a first father to exist objectively and are simultaneously deluded and comforted by it. A monotheistic god is not metaphysical but is a metaphorical problem, a subjective and imaginative artistic spoken and written word portrait that unfortunately is mistaken to exist objectively. Most humans want to increase their individual willing effort to exist. For some people and cultures, the only way to accomplish this personal goal is accept the existence of a monotheistic god who is imagined to have an all-powerful will in contrast to human free will which is feeble and mortal.

Adherents of monotheistic religions accept an external first father who will assist them to survive daily life and also death by resurrecting their physical body. Idolizing an external first father, monotheistic religions fail to recognize an internal animating soul of life. Monotheistic religions overlook evidence for a soul by focusing attention on a metaphorical first father god who will help them to survive.

The basis of the physical is not a metaphorical god as portrayed in story but is a real metaphysical seething sea of energy particles existing in an unseen dimension. What is real and animates life is a triune soul, yet while popularly and vaguely accepted to exist, it is not well known of what it may consist. Humankind in general has failed to discern a metaphysical animating soul to be a triune dynamic of hunger for food and water, sex and reproduction, and aggression. Humans have failed to discern the animating soul to be a continuation of recently discovered metaphysical energy particles of atoms and electrons, and to correctly ascertain that it is resistant to destruction and continues to exist in an afterlife dimension.

Sensed by many to exist in the physical body, is an energy that animates life and functions to survive. The sensed energy is an urging dynamic of hunger for food and water, sex and reproduction, and aggression. This urging presence is a less conscious and subconscious soul that through experience accumulates habit patterns to survive, and as a continuation of energy particles of the environment is long lasting and resistant to destruction.

Laying Down the Burden

Most people fear death while some look forward to the demise of the body as a laying down of the burden of life, of physical ailments and anxieties. Dying and death is eventually experienced by everyone. Everyone must someday lay down the burden of the physical body. The vast majority of people never attempt and therefore cannot complete the task of laying down the metaphysical burden of life through the practice meditative observation.

The existential task of reducing the burden of the conscious self by laying down some of its content is not so easy to do. Difficult while living to reduce excess conscious attention to sensations, and to reduce picture images made from them by the cerebral cortex of the brain. Most difficult of all is to reduce the burden of the dynamic subconscious soul urges of hunger for food, sex and reproduction, and aggression. As an animating dynamic that is a continuation of a sea of quantum energy particles of the environment, the soul is resistant to destruction and therefore is difficult to lay down the metaphysical burden.

The major task of life is not to reach a monotheistic god, which is just a metaphorical term for another dimension, but to reduce images and urges of a metaphysical habit pattern. Betwixt images and urges ever confined. The cerebral cortex of the brain transforms sensations from the senses into picture images. Some images are external and real from the senses, and some are subjective and artistic such as the tooth fairy, unicorns, and a monotheistic god. Both objective and subjective images are secondary to the primary dynamic urges of the soul, as a willing hunger for food, sex and reproduction, and aggression.

Not easy is it to release and lay down the burden of habit patterns of images and urges that function as a soul dynamic that lead to repetition and to another life existence. In stark contrast, the vast busy monotheistic majority of the earth's population think they need help to save their conscious personality and physical body, and therefore easily accept the offered metaphorical word art portrait of a first father god who will do the job for them.

Soul

The conscious self, the cerebral cortex of the brain, has the ability for picture images and reasoning and is often unimpressed by the less conscious and subconscious dynamic bodily urges of the soul. The soul is evident only in its effects, the beating of the heart and circulation, respiration, digesting of food, silent functioning of the immune system, and the healing of scratches and wounds.

These miracles are a dynamic not of conscious intention but a subconscious internal animating willing soul that is a continuation of the energy particles of the environment. Within the body there is a silent urging of a triune soul dynamic. In some parts of the body, there is an urging for food and water. In other parts there are forceful urgings for sex and reproduction, and in other parts urging for aggression.

The less conscious and subconscious knowing of the midbrain and body is an active soul dynamic to survive by urging and willing. This function prompts the conscious cerebral cortex to make picture images of objects in a space and time sequence as a way to better obtain what is needed to live. Conscious knowledge is often barely sufficient to guide innate subconscious knowing. Yet, the conscious self can train the less conscious and subconscious soul to want more or less of what is required of the necessities of food, sex and reproduction, and aggression. The conscious self can guide the subconscious soul to acquire various possessions and have preferred individual experiences.

Human life has always been, is, and will always be a competition. Conscious cerebral cortex picture images and word knowledge guide conscious willing behaviors to do, to have, or avoid. There is competition between the cerebral cortex of the brain, and the subconscious midbrain and body. Both conscious and subconscious functions compliment and also oppose each other. Human conscious and subconscious willing guided by a lack of sufficient knowledge is really problematic. Humans are seldom at peace, they are full of the animating essence of life, some good but just as much or more of evil willing and knowing.

The conscious cerebral cortex of the brain receives sensations and transforms them into picture images in a space and time sequence. This amazing ability contrasts with the less conscious and subconscious yet profound and seemingly numinous functions of midbrain and body that consist of willing urges for food and water, sex and reproduction, and aggression.

The subconscious soul is not as discriminating as is the conscious self of the cerebral cortex and wants what it urgingly desires despite what conscious knowledge and reason may want. If the subconscious soul wants what the conscious self does not, the triune soul frequently wins.

Save

Anecdotal accounts and case study evidence suggest that when the vital functions of the body cease, the animating willing soul exits and continues to survive saved by what it is, a continuation of energy. A monotheistic god is an ideated or imagined helper located in the cerebral cortex that diverts attention away from what truly animates life, the internal soul that is a continuation of energy particles of the environment. A cosmological force particlizes into particles, the smallest part of something. The force condenses into particles of energy that form the material (Latin mater, mother) support of the environment and continues internally as an animating willing dynamic of a triune soul of life.

The way to individual salvation is not through the willing of a first father god nor a god's son, nor through the combined helpful willing members of a religious group. The way to salvation both here and hereafter, is through use of the cerebral cortex to observe and moderate individual conscious and subconscious willing, and to remedy the deficiency or excess of hunger for food and water, sex and reproduction, and aggression.

Directing human behavior for the better can be subjectively and partially accomplished by appealing to the ideation of a first father god but is better done by observing and making adjustments to the subconscious soul, the real animating and willing culprit of existence. The subconscious soul is resistant to change as it consists of pragmatic willing urges and habit patterns of behaviors, mainly for food and water, sex and reproduction, and aggression. Only the conscious self of the cerebral cortex can save the individual from the subconscious recurring habit patterns of the animating and willing triune soul.

The conscious self of the cerebral cortex can save the individual from the soul, by observing and moderating its function as a cosmological default to survive. A subconscious soul saves the individual, and the conscious self can save the person from the soul.

Cerebral God

The monotheistic god of Judaism, Christianity, and Islam, represents an anxious concern and desperation of the human cerebral cortex of the brain to identify the origin of existence. The first father also represents a way to subjectively obtain help to survive life and death. The dictated commands of the monotheistic god are a help to determine what behaviors are right or wrong and good or evil. A first father is a way of comprehending the origin of existence, of rationalizing irrational experience, and a way of making life worthwhile.

Human concerns of life are portrayed in a symptomatic written word portrait of scripture as a monotheistic maker who dispenses reward and punishment. A monotheistic god is metaphorical not metaphysical, and is artistic not realistic. The story character is a metaphor that represents the cerebral cortex of the ideating brain. The metaphorical monotheistic god can only subjectively defend humans against a frequent havoc-wreaking environment of disasters, and the often troubling lower human midbrain and body behaviors.

The imprimatur of monotheistic religions is to worship a first father god. When worshipping the god, what really occurs is a taking of refuge in the ideating cerebral cortex of the brain that can imagine and produce the artistic spoken and written word portrait of a one and only first father. The conscious self artistically represents its existence as a higher role model of the god over the lower animating less conscious and subconscious midbrain and body, the triune willing urges of the soul which enables life to survive.

The cerebral cortex of a monotheistic adherent imagines a first father god who will save the individual after death by resurrecting the physical body to live again.

By so doing, the conscious cerebral cortex fails to observe that the willing efforts of the subconscious soul are saved as a continuation of the energy particles of a long-lasting environment that in turn are a continuation of the forceful momentum of a seemingly ever-lasting motion of the universe. The saving function of human life is not outside of an individual but is inside as an animating willing soul. Anecdotal and case study evidence suggests that individual conscious and subconscious willing patterns of both the self and soul survive death.

Problem of Willing

Methods and disciplines to direct human willing for the better are evident throughout history and vary with cultures. Hindu methods of dealing with human willing date to 3200 BCE and include the body disciplines of yoga and methods of meditation. The body postures or *asanas* discipline the subconscious willing of midbrain and body functions and muscles, while various meditation practices discipline conscious attention. Yoga ethics of behavior are the five *yamas* and *niyamas*, ten rules of what not to do and what the individual should do. Artistic visual depictions and verbal and written stories of various gods and goddesses did in the past and continue to serve as role models for Hindu willing behaviors.

A Hindu son by the name of Siddhartha Gautama (circa 623-543 BCE) clearly saw that life was problematic, and he set out to observe and to better comprehend it. Eventually, following six years of effort, at thirty-five years of age, Siddhartha became Buddha, meaning awake. He seems to have clearly perceived the main existential problem of human life to be willing. Humans have an ability to will both good and an excess use of force known as evil. To better comprehend and discipline willing, Buddha favored the older Hindu tradition of forest living and meditation. Seeking to awake requires limiting excessive participation in the distracting activities of daily life. The seclusion of forest living is a withdrawing from the busy and stressed lifestyles of family and society, and of nonparticipation in the accepted and sanctioned ignorance of a non-meditative lifestyle.

Through meditative observation, Buddha increased his knowledge of brain and body. He must have observed that knowledge is acquired through sensations of the senses, and these are then transformed into picture images. Sensations and picture images serve to guide the conscious and subconscious willing of behaviors. The essence of human life he found to be about willing for food and water, sex and reproduction, and aggression. Buddha must have eventually come to comprehend that these strong urges can and must be moderated. Not to do so results in the *dukkha* or sufferings of life. Through forest living and consistent meditation practice of training attention, Buddha moderated willing effort for sensations of:

Seeing
Hearing
Smelling
Tasting
Touching

He then proceeded to reduce his conscious willing efforts for picture images of:

Now
Past
Future

Meditation practice is a training to focus conscious and subconscious attention as a pragmatic way to reduce ideation, the cognitive placing of objects in a space and time sequence.

There must be a gradual moderating of conscious, less conscious, and subconscious residual effort to place objects in a space and time sequence. Meditation reduces attention to the internal sensations of external objects, calms attention to internal picture images of external objects, and moderates willing for the internal picture images of external objects. Cerebral cortex brain reality consists of a focus of attention and placing external objects in a subjective space and time sequence by internal conscious and subconscious willing effort.

The animating stimulus for this is the less conscious and mostly subconscious activity of hunger for food and water, sex and reproduction, and aggression.

The cerebral cortex of the brain makes picture images from sensations of the five sense organs and from external objects. Those who meditate reduce sensations from objects and reduce serial picture images that flood the conscious cerebral cortex of the brain. The sensate flood of picture images has an origin both in what is external and in what is internal as the urgings for food and water, sex, and aggression that lead to individual willing of success or failure, upliftment or downfall during life. Those who remove themselves from society meditate to reduce distractions and conflict with fellow humans and seek to develop the ability to observe and to better comprehend brain and body functions of life and death.

In the extant words attributed to Buddha, there are instructions on the practice of observant meditation but nowhere in the teachings is there an appeal to a monotheistic god to assist humans in their efforts to comprehend reality functions. Each person is tasked with doing the best they can with their individual willing efforts. The story of Buddha illustrates that life should be more about investigation of the human self and soul. He did not pursue a career in politics, banking, business, construction, or the arts. He taught the practice of training attention, close observation, and intuitive comprehension.

Legend tells that prior to his enlightenment, the princely Siddhartha Gautama was tempted by Mara, a figure who according to tradition represents death. Mara tempted the aspiring Buddha in two ways in an attempt to persuade him to give up his quest for enlightenment. Mara first brought his three beautiful daughters, who sought to distract and seduce him with sex. Secondly, Mara remarked to Siddhartha how thin he was from fasting, and tempted him to give up his quest and consume food. Siddhartha defeated Mara or death by refusing the temptation of sex, gradually began to eat food in moderation to regain his strength, and throughout the ordeal he did not react with overt aggression.

Just as with Buddha, sex and food distract individuals from observation and learning about life and death. Overly pursuing sex and over-indulging in consumption of food can be physically harmful, and at the very worse wastes valuable time by distracting from investigation of the human self and soul. All too quickly life ends, as death arrives sometimes expectedly but just as often unexpectedly to each individual. Some valuable time in life must be allotted to practice meditative observation and to learn about self and soul functions.

In a brief lifespan, little time is spent on attention to how the self transforms sensations into picture images of objects in space and time sequence of change, and how the triune soul functions as less conscious and subconscious willing urges for the survival of life. While personal experience is most valuable, anecdotal and case studies must also be considered as evidence that suggest the human soul survives death and oblivion.

Addiction

Humans are addicted to sensations, picture images, and to conscious and subconscious willing behaviors. Individual meditative practice is the existential task of focusing and calming conscious attention to sensations, and to reduce picture images of now, past, and future. The individual must moderate conscious and subconscious willing efforts of hunger for food, sex and reproduction, and aggression. To reduce strong habit patterns for picture images and for behaviors, is not so easy to do. Not an easy task to train the cerebral cortex of the brain to not make so many picture images, or to train the midbrain and body to moderate subconscious urges for food, sex, and aggression.

The discipline of meditation trains attention to stillness, and when supplemented with ascetic discipline of fasting limits daily food intake, assists in the limitation or elimination of sex, and limits aggression toward one's own body and others by a practice of compassion and love. The daily consistent practice of meditation can moderate the conditioned habit patterns for sensations, picture images, and excess willing behaviors for food, sex, and aggression.

For those who are unable to meditate, discipline, and moderate the addictions of life, the great majority accept the superficial addictive beliefs and traditions of a monotheistic religion. There are many individuals who find comfort in the subjective acceptance of an artistic word art portrait of a monotheistic god. Rabbis, priests and ministers, and imams, pedal the addictive spoken and written monotheistic word art to the marketplace customers of susceptible, vulnerable, and needy people.

Monotheistic Willing

The monotheistic religions of Judaism, Christianity, and Islam solve the problem of human willing by utilizing spoken and written word art to illustrate the portrait of a first father god. While this ploy is superficially effective for Middle East and western cultures, the word portrait of a first father god who dictates ethical and moral commands is artistic and not realistic. The word art portrait of a monotheistic god is a pragmatic but unrealistic way to deal with the existential problem of human willing.

The Genesis authors saw human willing to be a problem. Word artist scribes sought refuge in their creative ability to imagine and to write a story. The writers generated an artistic word portrait of story to direct human willing to what is good, the willing of a first father god. Throughout the Old Testament or Tanak, the god dictated 613 commandments that serve to direct human willing and thereby are intended to instill the good of social order. A strong-willed god is a way to increase or decrease individual human willing for good or evil behaviors. Sharing the story of a first father origin who dictates commands of thou shalt or thou shalt not, instills social order by directing and limiting individual willing to good and away from evil.

In contrast to Semitic culture, the Hindus developed methods of meditation with which to better observe and explore human brain and body functions. Biblical word artist story-tellers lacked methods and ways to obtain observational knowledge of the environment and the human brain and body.

Instead, the scriptural writers offered an ersatz subjective congestion of words, the word art story of a first father god. Biblical word artists generated subjective knowledge of story images to explain the beginning of existence to be a monotheistic first father god who dictates commands to direct human willing behaviors to what is good in life.

In the Middle East, the problem of where the environment and life come from was artistically solved by word artist scribes who creatively shaped the word portrait of a monotheistic god. The first father of Genesis is portrayed as breathing the will to live into the first human (2:7) and must have done the same for the second human. (2:21-23) The first humans were directed to exert their willing to cultivate the god's plants and trees for food. There was no willing by humans for sex and reproduction and aggression.

Willing is the problem of life, plainly seen after the first humans received their own free will and proceeded to use it to disobey the first father's will. The first humans also willfully obtained the god's stored knowledge from his fruit tree that endowed them with how to freely will for sex and reproduction and aggression.

When the first father breathed the breath of life into the first human, he also bestowed the willing movement of life within the body. The ability for willing was installed prior to bestowing a basic level of knowledge. The first human had only a basic intelligence, could only name things (Genesis 2:19-20) which occurs in human development from the toddler stage of eighteen months to three years of age.

The all-smart monotheistic god had knowledge of how to create the environment and life. The first father must also have known that when he breathed into the first human and endowed him with a free will to move and live, humans would then be free to obey or to disobey. Having a free will, the first humans freely ignored and disobeyed the first father, and separated themselves from what he wanted them to do or not do, namely, not to acquire more knowledge from his own special tree of knowledge.

The problem of life for humankind is the willing of one human against another, against other life forms, and against the willing-like change of the environment. The most difficult situation of willing, is internal individual conscious willing of the self against one's own less conscious and subconscious soul. As a continuation of and supported by the earth, the willing less conscious and subconscious midbrain and body evolved the cerebral cortex of conscious knowledge to artistically imagine a first father. The monotheistic god is credited with implanting the breath of life, alias the free will, alias the non-recognized animating soul.

The Christian gospels contain a number of ethical and moral teachings attributed to Jesus of Nazareth but just two commands direct willing. The individual is directed to willingly love a monotheistic first father and to love one's neighbors. (Mark 12: 28-34; Matthew 22: 36-40) To love a patriarchal god is to love what it subjectively represents, higher knowledge of the cerebral cortex of the brain where the idea originates. As a first father the god also represents the origin of midbrain and body functions of sexual and biological reproduction, and the authority of tradition as established by many deceased and living family fathers. To love a neighbor is to recognize a shared and common origin of a first father and the mutual ambivalent existential task and burden of willing the ever mixed good and evil experiences of life.

Life is a struggle to obtain what is good and to avoid evil. There is a struggle between good and evil within humans, between the cerebral cortex of the brain or conscious self, and the midbrain and body as the dynamic subconscious soul. Within humans there is a struggle of a good reasoning cerebral cortex of the brain with the evils of midbrain and body and its nonreasoning urges of hunger for food, sex and reproduction, and aggression. Internally, the cerebral cortex of brain and midbrain and body conflict, is externalized and represented as the duality of a good monotheistic god and an opposing evil Satan or Devil.

God and Human Will

The monotheistic god's will, is free to will both good and evil, and if not he would not be free. The first father passed along a milder or smaller version of his free will to the first humans who were made in his image. (Genesis 1:26-27) Human willing was and is free to will the good of obedience and the evil of disobedience. The first father willed some of his good and evil knowledge into a tree, and also banished and inflicted curses of evil to punish humans with the struggle and suffering of life.

Chapter 1 of Genesis idolizes the greater willing the monotheistic god who willed the all "good" of existence. (Genesis 1:31) Unfortunately, the first father also freely endowed humans with a free will like his own good and evil capable free will and this act set the stage for the sin of separation. Christian original sin occurred when the first father made a human free will similar to his own and placed it within the first humans who soon freely opposed him with it. The Genesis first father's will, is faulty. This is obvious as a distinction first formed within the god as the twin ability for good and also evil, and both traits are first expressed only by the monotheistic god in his willing behaviors and knowledge. The god willfully breathed a minor version of his own evil capable will into the first humans who then proceeded to use their free willing ability for the behavioral evil of disobedience that caused a sin (Hebrew hata, separation) of separation from the first father.

An unavoidable conclusion drawn from the metaphorical Genesis story is that humans received a faulty evil capable will from the good and evil willing of the monotheistic god. A story separation occurred between the metaphorical first father and the free-willing first humans. Willing struggle of differences continue today for real between family members, friends, and fellow humans. The young of today continue to willfully follow in their ancestor's footsteps.

Having imparted a lesser version of his own evil capable free will to the first humans, the god then willed a second evil on the earth when he placed some of his evil knowing in his special tree of both good and evil knowledge.

The god also later willed his third evil act when he cursed and inflicted harsh punishment upon the first humans with the many evils of life. (Genesis 3:14-19)

The evil knowledge willed into a special tree by the first father, compounded the prior human free will ability the first humans acquired from the god to freely will the evil of disobedience and to go their separate ways. The existential problem of life is that having the god-endowed ability to freely will the good of obedience or the evil of disobedience, is joined with good and evil knowledge acquired from the god's own tree which exacerbates the human condition. The obtaining of good and evil knowledge from the god's tree by the first humans, compounded the innate good and evil capable free will breathed into humans by the good and evil free will of a first father god. The first father freely can and does will either good or evil, and since human free will was made in the god's image, (Genesis 1:26-27) then humans just like the first father also freely will both good and evil. Ever since the Genesis of the environment and life by the god, all humans thereafter take after their metaphorical pops.

Made in the image of the first father god with an evil capable free will, the first humans wanted and obtained more knowledge for themselves but unfortunately, just like their free will, it also contained evil. The first humans simply wanted more knowledge but their first father failed to provide them with a tree of knowledge that was at least predominantly good or all good. The first father could not have made a tree of all good knowledge, as the tree of good and evil knowledge he made, accurately reflects his own limited and dualistic free will and knowledge for both good and evil. The artistic imagined story character of a good monotheistic god, really represents the evolved conscious cerebral cortex that attempts to control the evil urges of the less conscious and subconscious midbrain and body, a real dynamic of a hunger for food and water, sex and reproduction, and aggression.

Good is the conscious willing of the cerebral cortex of the brain, while evil is the less conscious and subconscious willing of midbrain and body.

Biological urges of hunger for food, sex and reproduction, and aggression, easily get out of control and this usually leads to conflict between the cerebral cortex of the brain versus the midbrain and body. In other words, the conscious self, conflicts with the not recognized but real less conscious and subconscious animating and willing triune soul.

Das Ville

The German philosopher Arthur Schopenhauer (1788-1860) made the statement that art is beneficial to humans as it bestows a temporary respite in life from the "penal servitude of willing." In his seminal work, *The World as Will and Representation*, Schopenhauer discusses three ways of dealing with human willing through the use of:

Art
Ethics
Asceticism

Willing is the existential problem of life, and for Schopenhauer, art suspends willing for brief minutes and hours of time. Eventually, after attention has been drawn to and captivated by the aesthetic beauty of an artistic work of music, story, sculpture, or visual art, mundane life resumes with willing efforts to resolve the difficulties of existence. There are existential willing struggles between conscious and subconscious within the individual, with other humans, other life forms, and with the willing-like non-conscious changes of the environment.

Ethics, the study of value judgements of what is right or wrong, good or evil, and the doing of what is good, has its rewards but only partially solves the problem of human willing. Ethics guides conscious attention to willing good and away from evil but it is often difficult to determine what the outcome of particular behaviors may be. Ethics does not reduce the human less conscious and subconscious willing soul that is resistant to destruction, it purifies and guides it into more acceptable social behaviors and outcomes.

Reduction of the intensity of human willing for either good or evil requires mild to moderate asceticism. Ascetic practices include meditation to discipline conscious attention, and various exercises such as yoga, weight training, walking, jogging, a healthy diet, and fasting to discipline the body. Moderate asceticism limits, disciplines, and reduces distracting and frivolous ways of willing existence. Ascetic discipline focuses attention to better examine brain and body functions so as to better comprehend the willing functions of the conscious self and the subconscious soul.

Those who retreat to a monastery, seminary, or ashram for some time, seek an increase of comprehension and peace. Some accept the monotheistic tradition that the repository of greater knowledge and peace resides with an external monotheistic god. Other individuals do not seek to make the acquaintance of a first father but instead make the effort to calm attention so as to better observe and to comprehend the internal cerebral cortex and midbrain and body functions. Both monotheists and non-monotheists practice asceticism as a way to better discipline the conscious self and less conscious and subconscious soul functions.

The animating soul is a continuation of an external seething sea of energy particles of the environment and is an internal triune dynamic of willing hunger for food and water, sex and reproduction, and aggression. The use of ascetic limitations reduces and moderates the usually excess willing of these triune functions.

The conscious self can master the less conscious and subconscious soul by moderating urges for food, sex, and aggression that fuel the production of picture images and excess attention and behaviors for sensate objects. Willing for aesthetic experiences, for what is ethically and morally good and avoiding what is evil, and ascetic discipline of conscious and subconscious willing, brings relative happiness and some occasional moments of sublime peace.

Pragmatic Willing

The God & Soul Theory serves as a pragmatic tool in directing human willing to what is better in life. The theory asserts that the much-vaunted monotheistic god of Middle East and western culture, is a spoken and written work of word art. A first father is a metaphorical attempt to solve the problem of the innate duality of human willing of the conscious self, and the subconscious triune soul willing of hunger for food and water, sex and reproduction, and aggression. These evolved differing dynamics of willing contribute to individual confusion as to what is best to will for in life, and this poignant experience produced the ideation of a first father god and monotheistic religions. The God & Soul Theory advocates a pragmatic willing to direct the conscious self and subconscious soul to what is better in four areas of life:

Health
Knowledge
Work and Financial Security
Relationships

Time is limited in life and there is only so much of it available to develop health, learning and knowledge, work and financial security, and the cultivation of loving supportive relationships. While existence is limited and remains incomplete in many ways, the challenge is to reduce lack and excess and to complete these four areas of willing as much as is possible. Everyone is in various stages of incompleteness and completeness in these four areas of life. The individual challenge is to complete life the best that one knows how and to the pragmatic extent of individual ability.

Existence

Conscious attention and sensations of the senses change from second to second, as do fleeting picture images of now, past, and future. Human conscious willing is changeable and free to do or not to do, and often is only partial or not effective. A monotheistic god represents the higher attitude humans can adopt about their precarious existential experience of fleeting sensations, changing picture images, and oftentimes ineffectual willing for and against situations.

During a lifetime, sooner or later most individual end in a bad way. What dooms an individual to an early death may be illness, injury, depression, or aggression. If able to reach old age, the sense organs and memory deteriorate, as do muscles of the body. It is a hope of many people that a monotheistic god will save them, either in life or after death during a body resurrection. Praying to a first father who can assist and remedy situations, is an appeal to a subjective artistic imagined story character. The only real support in the struggle of living is that of family, friends, and members of monotheistic groups who render assistance and comfort to each other during times of need.

For many people, if there were not at least a subjective monotheistic god, humankind would be stuck in the existential mire of life, the less conscious and subconscious animating soul dynamic of a hunger for food and water, sex and reproduction, and aggression. Daily experiencing the forceful willing urges of the triune soul, the conscious cerebral cortex of vast numbers of people forsake the idea of a monotheistic god and instead surrender to the primal midbrain and body functions. For the throng, conscious knowledge and education-supplemented willing take a back seat to less conscious and subconscious knowledge and willing functions of the soul.

Supplement

Worship of a monotheistic god is a subjective ideational support during the existential life situations of angst and despair. A first father god is a subjective mental supplement to boost the determination and strength of individual willing and thereby alleviate frustrating and painful experience. The word supplement is defined as:

"Something added to complete, to make up for a deficiency of a diet or written work. To add or supply, to make better, sufficient, or whole such as health or comprehension."

The real willing-like change of the environment, and the inner subconscious willing urges of a triune soul of hunger for food and water, sex and reproduction, and aggression.

These are the *raison d'etre* for the subjective acceptance of a strong willing monotheistic god to supplement the weaker willing and knowing of humans. A larger than life first father is an ideational subjective supplement, a match opponent to the greater size of the earth, sun, and immense universe. The artistic word portrait of a monotheistic god is a supplement to ease the real fears of living and dying.

Authority figures supplement their rule with a monotheistic god as a way to obtain obedience, social order, and money from adherents. The willing of a monotheistic god supplements and makes human willing worthwhile, and adds worth to oftentimes worthless human efforts. With life supplemented by a monotheistic god, many humans can then go about the daily challenging tasks of living, confident and encouraged they are protected by a strong willing first father.

Ever Changing

Sensations of the senses change from second to second, and picture images of now past, and future change from moment to moment. What endures for such a brief time cannot be worth very much. Conscious willing is also changeable and can do or not do, please or displease in an instant. Some people accept the existence of a monotheistic god who is longer lasting and who has a stronger willing ability. An artistic imagined word portrait of a first father who lasts through all time can assist the devoted who are disoriented by ever-changing time. A monotheistic god who is eternal or unchanging is an artistic ideation, as a way to endure the existential change of second to second sensations and picture images of now, past, and future, and changeable willing efforts occurring in an inexorable sequence of time.

Observing how sensations, picture images, and conscious willing continually change, can easily lead to existential angst, dissociation, and despair. What may uplift an individual attitude is an often vague sensing of a less conscious and subconscious willing that is longer lasting and enduring.

Human conscious willing to exert more or less effort to do or accomplish, if often repeated, forms enduring subconscious habit patterns that repeat and are resistant to change and destruction. The commonly accepted enduring will of a monotheistic god only reflects and represents the human will that is resistant to destruction by changing time. To the busy conscious self, there is often not enough or there is too much time in a day, night, or a lifetime. For the timeless, long-lasting, and resistant to destruction soul, time is but a piddling trifle of pleasures and pains.

The internal willing behavior of life survives dependent on the external supportive behaviors of the environment. Life exists dependent on the internal willing behaviors of the less conscious and subconscious soul urgings of hunger for food and water, sex and reproduction, and aggression of the human body. The behavior of life is not related to the story behavior of a monotheistic god but is a relative function of the willing-like behavior of a real changing environment. In turn, all behaviors of the environment and life are relative behaviors of the willing-like behavior of a wholistic universe, and probably of an even more immense multiverse.

Forces, energy, material, and living forms of existence display willing-like behaviors, many of which are repetitive and are construed by humans to be laws. However, laws belong to gods and humans and all environmental and living forms only exhibit behaviors, not laws. If these behaviors are observed by humans to be consistent and reliably repetitive, they are then said to be laws (Latin *lex*, Indo-European *leg*, to speak) but this is a misnomer as only gods and humans speak and write laws.

The animating behavior of life, the soul, has a cosmological origin, and therefore wants to continue to go and to grow forward in space and time. The willing soul expands just as does the observed behavior of the universe. Energy and unseen dimensions of existence are the super nature of reality, as are the dynamic energetic particles of the earth and sun environment that in a sense, will life to exist and continue.

Awash in a sea of energy particles, life is a continuation of and is supported by the willing-like change and behavior of the environment that assembles, disassembles, and reassembles existence. The environment consists of behavior patterns that are repeated, such as cycles of the sun and moon, day and night, seasons, and weather.

Human life consists of habit patterns of behavior that are a continuation of energy. Following death, as anecdotal and case study evidence suggests, the human triune soul may continue to exist in a dimension to where it transits and may return to life. Repetitive willing behaviors of life establish a pattern of conscious and subconscious habits. As a local continuation of energy particles and a supportive nonlocal ground of unparticlized cosmological force and dimensional reality, human habits are reserved and probably preserved.

Habit Pattern

Human conscious attention is conditioned and directed to what is outside of the body but is seldom trained to observe what occurs inside. A focus of meditative attention on the internal sensation of breathing calms distraction to external sensations, picture images, and calms conscious and subconscious willing that stimulate images of what is most wanted in life, food and water, sex and reproduction, and aggression.

The conscious cerebral cortex of the brain is bombarded with brief sensations and picture images that change from moment to moment. Focusing attention on the now sensation of breathing observes a usually unnoticed and less conscious and subconscious willing for air. Meditative focus of conscious attention to breathing leads to comprehension that subconscious willing animates the body to live and survive.

The soul is a triune function of willing urges for air, food and water, sex and reproduction, and aggression, a dynamic supported by and rooted in energy particles of the earth and sun environment.

The conscious self learns fast while the less conscious and subconscious soul learns much slower but is longer lasting as habit patterns. Less conscious and subconscious willing behaviors form habit patterns that resist alteration and degrading of them. Unobserved and unresolved, strong willing habits to survive remain during life and after death and as anecdotal and case study evidence suggest, continue to exist and can also recur. Subconscious urges of willing for sensations and conscious picture images of now, memory, and the future, and also less conscious dream images tend to continue.

Not an external monotheistic god but it is what exists in the body as subconscious urges that is the soul and that form repetitive habit patterns that are long-lasting and resistant to destruction. Human habit patterns are a continuation of the repeating external behaviors of the environment and its habit-like cycles of day and night, and seasons, sun, stars, moon and ocean tides. The universe functions through repetition of behavior patterns of circles and cycles and humans are a continuation of them as conscious, less conscious, and subconscious repetitive willing habit patterns.

Will the universe someday cease to expand and to exist? The answer is unknown as no human will live so long to observe the phenomenon of a cosmos that ceases to exist. Since the human self and soul are a continuation of the ever-forceful and expanding cosmos, the same question can be posed about the dynamic of them both. Human willing is resistant to destruction and is metaphorically represented as such by the story of a monotheistic god.

The exaggerated powerful will of a mythic first father, really represents human will that is resistant to destruction as it is a continuation of the will-like change of energy particles of the environment. The importance of the human will is neglected in monotheistic religions, except to say it is free and yet mortal as the god must resurrect it along with the breath or spirit, and the body.

Monotheistic religions favor an external willing of a first father patriarchal progenitor who may save some humans and not others.

What really saves an individual is an animating soul that following death, exits a physical body and earth dimension to exist as an ethereal habit pattern of willing to reside in a near-earth halo or dimension of energy. The artistic story image of a strong ever-existing monotheistic god is a vicarious way an individual can exist and live again during a future resurrection. This is an artistic portrayed external mechanism versus an internal real animating willing soul.

Evidence suggests that some near-death experiences may be real events of disembodied survival, and these anecdotal accounts and case studies of the phenomenon suggest the probability of a real afterlife dimension. The evidence for some residual survival of what animates life, consists of childhood reincarnation memories, comforting after death visits by deceased relatives and friends, sightings and sensing of ghosts, and double-blind experiments of evidential mediums.

Willing Groove

Human willing is often ineffective and knowledge may be lacking to direct it for the better. The body eventually wears out and must die but anecdotal reports and case studies suggest the willing pattern of a subconscious soul may continue and not go into oblivion. Willing consists of good and bad behaviors that tend to repeat as subconscious habits and are accompanied by some conscious picture images as spacetime guides. Habits vary but are a pattern of conscious, less conscious, and subconscious willing urges mainly for food and water, sex and reproduction, and aggression.

Sensations change from second to second, while picture images of now, past, and future do likewise. Conscious willing is changeable but less conscious and subconscious willing can change but is longer lasting as it is capable of forming habit patterns. Humans are only free to follow the habitual grooves of what the environment provides for them, and are free to move through life only along the determining grooves of genetic and biological functions. Evidence suggests that humans are only free to follow the willing conscious and subconscious grooved patterns of behaviors acquired during life.

Like a 45 or 78 rpm record, or a CD or DVD, humans are unknowingly free to follow set grooves to play and to replay. Since the animating soul is a dynamic continuation of atom, electron, and subatomic quantum energy particles of the environment, it is therefore resistant to destruction.

Humans are connected to the dimension of the earth through the dimension of energy particles, and where there are at least two real dimensions, there is a probability that other real supportive dimensions exist that humans are connected to. As a continuation of energy, anecdotal and case study evidence suggests that behavior patterns of the soul may be saved as some residual conscious images and mostly subconscious willing efforts to a field dimension afterlife, and as such may return to live again.

Spirit and Soul

Christian authority figures of the twenty-first century, have been observed to use the word soul as a referent for what survives physical death. The glaring discrepancy is, there is no mention of a soul in monotheistic scriptures. Monotheistic tradition is that of an animating spirit or breath (Latin *spiritus*, breath; Hebrew *ruach*, breath) obtained from a monotheistic god. In the Garden of Eden story, willing movement of the human body was endowed by a first father breathing into the first human. (Genesis 2:7)

Monotheistic religions are soulless and rely on a monotheistic god to resurrect a soulless body that contains a mortal non-metaphysical breath or spirit, and a mortal free will, both of which must be reattached to the body during a resurrection. A super monotheistic god breathing a free will of bodily movement into the first human, is a metaphorical way of saying there is something super about human willing but the insight is ignored and not followed up on its importance. The first father animated the first human body with a breath, alias a free will to live and move. This momentous event of an animating breath and free will, direct from the first father, is portrayed as not special, not long-lasting, and as not resistant to destruction.

The breath and free will are portrayed as mortal and must be restored to a resurrected body by the god. The story detail is a real travesty as it obscures a real internal triune soul by misdirecting attention from the environment to the artistic story character of a monotheistic first father god.

Self and Soul

Self is subservient to soul. While the conscious self and its ability to transform sensations into spacetime picture images is an astounding feat, it will ever remain subservient to the subconscious soul that animates life to survive as willing urges of hunger for food and water, sex and reproduction, and aggression.

Supported by the best evidence of neuroscience, the number of brain neurons total approximately eighty-six billion. Of this amount, the cerebral cortex of the brain or conscious self, consists of sixteen billion neurons and is approximately fourteen percent of total brain neurons. The midbrain consists of seventy billion neurons and is eighty-six percent less conscious and subconscious soul functions of the autonomic nervous system of the body. This fact suggests a realistic extrapolation of what may possibly survive physical death. The surviving soul partially retains the habit of making conscious picture images but consists mostly of subconscious habits of behavior as triune willing urges of hunger for food and water, sex, and aggression.

Conscious knowledge and willing generally dominate attention. When conscious knowledge is lacking, there is a predominance of willing and knowing urges of the less conscious and subconscious dynamic of hunger for food, sex, and aggression. The physical correlation of the triune dynamic soul function, includes the intestinal tract and circulatory system to distribute nutrition and liquids, the genitals for sex and reproduction, and muscles for mobility and aggression.

The three Fs of the triune soul are "feeding, fucking, and fighting."

The three Fs are the dominant and essential behaviors of life as hunger for food, sex and reproduction, and aggression. These dynamic traits and behaviors more than any others, enable individual life to survive. The soul is a subconscious autonomic function of the midbrain and body that knows how to animate the heart to beat, to digest and absorb food and water, and move the lungs to breathe, and grows the body, hair, and fingernails.

The soul is a continuation of external energy particles of the willing-like changing environment. In turn, the local environment is a continuation of the seemingly infinite willing-like cosmological nonlocal motion of the universe. Individual human effort is a local exertion that is a continuation of a nonlocal exertion that moves the universe. Life is an animated continuation of energy particles of the environment, and this fact suggests individual survival following death.

For some time now, monotheistic religions have praised a monotheistic god whose willing is said to be eternal and not destructible. To write a story of an imagined first father who is then exaggerated to be a god who is the origin of humankind is to belittle the significance and cosmological importance of human willing. The story character god's inflated omnipotent willing is a metaphor that represents a real human willing soul that is resistant to destruction. The human body is eventually destroyed but not its animating essence, its less conscious and subconscious willing for food and water, sex and reproduction, and aggression. Anecdotal and case study evidence suggests the triune soul survives life and death by willing subconscious habit patterns of behaviors and also some enduring picture images.

The three traditional attributes of a monotheistic god are, omnipotent, omnipresent, and omniscient. The attributes of a monotheistic god are touted as, omnipotent or all powerful, omniscient or all knowing, and omnipresent or everywhere present. The reality is, an omnipotent god of monotheism is really a subjective impotent idea, and the notion of an omniscient first father represents only human nescience.

To round out the three attributes, the supposed omnipresent monotheistic god is really only locally existent in the human cerebral cortex of the human brain and resides in no other place.

It is really a human willing soul that while not all powerful, has some attribute of omnipotence as it is resistant to destruction. A human willing soul is omnipresent as it is a continuation of a seemingly infinite field of energy particles, related to movement and growth of all life and the cosmological motion of the universe. It is omniscient or all-knowing is it knows how to continue and not cease to exist, and how to animate life. The subconscious soul has also evolved the conscious self or cerebral cortex of the brain that can observe and if motivated and disciplined can comprehend how to bring it to a quiescence and ending.

While evidence suggests that the animating soul survives death, it cannot save the body. To save the body is why a monotheistic first father god is imagined in a word portrait story who will resurrect it. Unfortunately, the artistic imaginal idea of a willing god conceals an animating willing human soul that continues to this day to not be recognized by monotheistic religions. Even though humans are made in the image of a monotheistic god who endowed them with a free will, monotheistic religions portray the human will as inert and destructible at the time of death.

For the followers of Judaism and Islam, there is no willing human soul, only the willing of a physical body and its resurrection. For Christians, a first father breathed a breath of life (Latin spiritus, breath) into humans. (Genesis 2:7) Christians see the spirit or breath of life to be good, has some intelligence, and is worthy of being saved. Luke 23:46 has Jesus saying on the cross, "...Father, into thy hands I commend my spirit...." (Hebrew *ruach*, breath; Latin *spiritus*, breath) Christians look forward to their breath and free will to be saved and reattached to their reassembled body during a future resurrection. Such silly superstition is really a monotheistic metaphor for a real animating human soul that exists as a continuation of a seething sea of energy particles of the environment.

Difference

There is a difference between the Old and New Testaments of the bible on the topic of death. The glaring obvious difference is that in the Old Testament, when the body, free will and breath cease, they don't travel anywhere. They disperse and return to Sheol or the earth until resurrected by the first father god. In the New Testament, Early Christianity insists that after death, the physical body of Jesus was resurrected and soon transported to the first father god. (Luke 24:51) The body of less qualified followers of Jesus can also expect to be resurrected at some unknown time in the future. Later Christians insist they possess an animating breath (Latin spiritus) or spirit that survives along with some sort of personality and goes to a heaven dimension. At a future unknown time, the body will be resurrected and the free will and breath or spirit will be rejoined with it on the earth.

Both Old and New Testament biblical views are in error as the views fail to recognize that a first father god is metaphorical and not metaphysical. Both views fail to recognize the existence of an animating soul that is a continuation of the energy particles of the earth which bestows a resistant to destruction. For Christians, a first father represents relief from the strife of life to an afterlife dimension to which the breath (Latin spiritus) or spirit transits followed by a future resurrection of the physical body. Christianity is correct in pointing out the existence of an afterlife dimension of existence but anecdotal reports and case study evidence suggests a differing with how it is often portrayed in popular Christian belief and tradition.

Relief

Fragile life is observed to consist of good experiences and daily routines performed against a background of potential accident, illness, ageing, and death. Awareness of this on some level taints good experiences, and may often cast a dim pallor that distorts life and leads to noncaring and evil human behaviors. Some even find it more feasible to will death than that which one cannot or stubbornly does not want to will for.

How can something exist within humans that is resistant to destruction when the body is vulnerable, dysfunctional, ages, dies, and decays. Recently harvested food must be kept in a refrigerator to prevent its rapid decay and consumption by mold and bacteria. For many people, one subjective particular concept relieves and brightens the dismal aspects of life as little can; this is the artistic story that simplifies and misidentifies the origin of existence to be a monotheistic god.

Twenty-five hundred years ago in the primitive past of the Middle East, superstition, lack of intelligence and knowledge, and artistic ability combined in a few individuals to produce the Genesis word portrait story of a monotheistic god. Ever since, much monotheistic blabber and word nonsense has been written and spoken about a first father god. Members of monotheistic religions find refuge in a subjective remedy for existence, the concocted ideational pill of a first father god swallowed by many as a way to find relief from life and death.

A portrait of a monotheistic god sketched only with words of story, suffices to bring the relief of belief to many. A first father is a bright spark of subjective good in a real day and night reality of good and evil experiences. The portable idea there is an exclusive good of a monotheistic fatherly god beyond all other fathers is easily utilized by recalling it as needed to relieve discomfort and despair. Basking in the subjective ideation of a first father god as a way to reduce fear and anxiety, some individuals share the idea and join with others for mutual support in monotheistic group worship.

Curse

A curse is defined as:

"To swear, wish, appeal or pray to a supernatural power to cause evil or misfortune to befall someone or something."

Christians blame the first humans for the original sin of separation from the monotheistic god as told in the biblical Garden of Eden story.

Yet this is undeserved as the god endowed the first humans with a free will not unlike his own, that can freely do or not do as a situation arises and varies.

Any fault humans have, comes from a first father who represents many forefathers who have always insisted on willing for sex and bringing children into existence, and who then until their dying day must of necessity hunger for food and express aggression. Not a story first father but many real forefathers continue to curse their progeny with the sentence of life and death through sexual reproduction, Monotheistic religions see the suffering of life as a curse from a metaphorical relative, a first father god. The real curse of life is inflicted by many forefathers and mothers whose behavior in wanting and willing to experience the intense pleasure of orgasm, often results in sexual reproduction. The monotheistic word art of a first father god is a poor attempt to ameliorate life. Many people of the past and those living today have conspired, are complicit, and guilty in the fraud of accepting a monotheistic god to be objective when it is really a subjective word art portrait. Feh and ptui!

While only good exists in the book of Genesis chapter 1, the evil of existence arrives in chapters 2 and 3. The metaphorical origin of evil begins when the good first father gave the first humans a good and evil capable free will like his own, capable of both good and evil as the freedom to do or not to do, to obey or not obey. This is the first metaphorical appearance of evil in the Genesis story. From the good and evil free will of the first father the second mention of evil occurs when the god willed his tree of good and evil knowledge into existence. Using their good and evil capable free will, the first humans wanted the good and evil knowledge to complete the suite of life.

The first father god inflicted the first curse on humans by covertly bestowing a free will that can do or not do, and agree or disagree. To have a free will is a real curse as it easily leads to differences, conflict, and aggression. The second curse is overt, that of providing some of his knowledge for the first humans to obtain, which of necessity is both good and evil.

Knowledge is often lacking or incomplete, and behaviors and their future consequences are often unknown. The third overt curse is multifaceted, and consists of struggle between male and female, with animals, and to survive obtaining food in the environment. (Genesis 3:14-19)

The Genesis monotheistic word portrait of a first father god is a metaphorical artistic attempt of story to subjectively explain and by so doing, to reduce the curse that is life. Forget about really removing the curse of life inflicted by the metaphorical first father. The fairytale god ideated by the cerebral cortex has not done much of anything, aside from a subjective placebo effect, to reduce the curse of human suffering.

Many people who lack individual ability and assistance from fellow humans, may be persuaded to subjectively accept the objective existence of a monotheistic god who will help them to reach success and reduce the curse of sickness, ignorance, poverty, and a lack of supportive, trusting, and loving relationships. The Middle East artistic word art story of a monotheistic god is a subjective way to feel more comfortable with the curse of life by having the imagined company of a first father. The monotheistic oriented cerebral cortex of the brain poorly attempts to solve the problem of life with a word art story of a first father in an attempt to reduce what many see as the curse of existence.

Therefore, the cerebral cortex of the human brain had to evolve to develop the sciences as real ways of reducing and saving humans from an accursed life. Only science can assist in relieving some of the real curses of life which include poor health and injury, lack of knowledge, lack of work and financial security, and lack of supportive loving relationships. The curse of living can be at least reduced, and with time removed by making efforts to improve life experience. Most achieve some of these four goals in life but find it difficult to attain success in all of them.

Life Remedy

The remedy of monotheistic religions for life is not to be alone but to have the ideated company of a first father god. A monotheistic god is a false yet pragmatic way of feeling good about the many not so good experiences of life and death. Accepting the good of a first father who intends human life to exist, affirms and makes later human sexual reproduction, living, and dying worthwhile.

The imagined bright spot of a first father represents an affirmation of sexual reproduction by many forefathers. Life has not been intended by an external rational god but is intended by an internal and irrational animating willing soul of hunger for food and water, sex and reproduction, and aggression that is a continuation of the orderly but nonrational energy elements of the environment. Accepting a monotheistic god to exist brings some relief to an individual that life is okay and under control.

For monotheistic religions, humans must struggle through the many evils of life afflicted by curses and guilt traced back to an act of primal disobedience in the Garden of Eden. Since then, humans have an ambivalence of patriarchal love, fear, and hate for the first father who cursed and punished the first humans and all descendants daily from then on. Rather than the subjective word portrait of a monotheistic god, what humans should realistically dislike and hate is the biological curse of sexual desire and lust of many forefathers that has brought so many children into existence to struggle and suffer grievously. Human life comes from many willing forefathers, reduced in the Genesis story to one symbolic character of a first father.

The unobserved yet imagined all-powerful conscious willing of a monotheistic god is preferred over the observable real act of biological reproduction and the subconscious willing of a triune soul as hunger for food and water, sex, and aggression. Accepting the subjective idea of a first father that is imagined to exist beyond the extended line of many previous biological forefathers, relieves worries, redeems, and makes sexual reproduction and struggle of life worthwhile. A greater good is subjectively imagined to exist and is identified as a first father that exists beyond spacetime.

Worship of a conscious and rational god is really an artistic response to a real animating subconscious and irrational willing urge for sex and reproduction. The artistic word portrait of a first father is a monotheistic fib that represents real countless acts of sexual reproduction by many forefathers through distant time. The subjective idea of a first father in which many have faith and trust, simply represents one shared origin of sexual reproduction.

Striving to identify the origin of existence, the attention of biblical word artist scribes eventually landed on the beginning of many previous fathers and creatively imagined it to be a monotheistic god. The words that tell a story of a first father god represents a shift of attention away from a real origin of human sexual intercourse and reproduction and the supportive earth, to an artistic spoken and written word portrait. This distraction of misplaced attention to a god suffices for the terminal easily convinced.

The word story of a monotheistic god artistically misrepresents where existence comes from. Where life really comes from is the wordless less conscious, and subconscious internal willing of an animating triune soul as urges of hunger for food and water, sex and aggression that is a continuation of the nonword using environment. Human origin is not a first father god but is a long line of shared willing by forefathers for sexual reproduction as a continuation of a supportive sea of energy particles of the environment. A monotheistic god exists only in the never-never land of human ability to artistically imagine fictional stories. A first father is an artistic attempt of the conscious cerebral cortex of the human brain to dominate the environment, and to direct human less conscious and subconscious behaviors of the midbrain and body, the dynamic of which is an animating and willing soul.

Many find refuge and relief in the essential behaviors of life, the consuming of food, sex and reproduction, and aggression. Short term pleasures temporarily relieve the discomforts and struggles of living, yet the frequent repetition of them easily becomes monotonous and painful ennui.

The sensate pleasures of life are fleeting, and many people therefore flock to the subjective idea of what can bring about relief and give individuals what they want. The artistic answer to the question of what can alleviate suffering, for monotheistic adherents, is a first father of many fathers who will help and provide relief to any deserving, unfortunate, and needy childlike adult.

Much to his everlasting credit, Buddha (circa 623-543 BCE) announced that life does suffer but not from the curse of a monotheistic god. Life suffers from the environment, and from its functional parts that eventually dysfunction. Buddha reduced the curse of life by eating one meal daily, did not have sex, and meditated on developing compassion. This ascetic practice reduced and moderated the curse of life, of hunger for food, se and reproduction, and aggression, and led him to experience Nirvana. Buddha found that even death may not remove the curse of individual life and death, as humans may reincarnate to live again.

Willing

Humans are capable of willing what is good and also what is evil. The ability to will both, according to the Genesis story, began long ago when the first father endowed the first human with a free will not unlike his own. Endowed with an evil capable free will, the first humans then willed other than what their first father willfully told them not to do and obtained the god's own good and evil knowledge from his fruit tree. Humans obtained both their good and evil capable will, and their good and evil knowledge from the good and evil first father god. Therefore, humans must use their marred will as they do for both good and evil, ordained by the will and knowledge of their own mighty parental figure.

Human existence is cursed by the first father as portrayed in the biblical Genesis story. (3:14-19) Unnoticed and not commented on, the very first real curse of existence is in what the first humans obtained from the first father. The god endowed humans with a lesser copy of his own marred ability to will both good and evil as evident by the good and evil knowledge he placed in a tree and its fruit.

This is of course, an artistic metaphor that illustrates that humans have a real evolved higher conscious cerebral cortex of the brain capable of picture image knowledge of reasoning, and have a lower subconscious knowledge of the midbrain and body. The midbrain and body contain innate knowledge that consists of biological urges of a triune soul of hunger for food and water, sex and reproduction, and aggression. This innate knowledge is the real curse of existence, a dynamic passed down not from a first father but from many forefathers.

The opening chapters of the metaphorical Genesis story tell how the first humans failed the first father and thereby separated themselves from what good the god could do for them. Humans have been separating themselves from what is good ever since the primal separation from the god. The good of existence is not all good as the monotheistic god has both a good and evil free will and good and evil knowledge. Humans share in this metaphorical hereditary legacy. Humans have failed to do and be all good and are blamed while the first father god is absolved of all blame, of having both a marred evil capable will and evil knowledge. Humans have not failed and are not separate from a monotheistic god except by a story timeline.

According to the Genesis story, humans are deemed to be separate from, have failed to be close with, and are shunned by an all good first father. The god seems to shun most of the population, except for a few *uber mensch* or saints who manage to sublimate and subdue their evil impulses and are then favored by the all good god. The real human fault is not theological but physiological and psychological, caused in part by the evolved cerebral cortex of the brain composed of sixteen billion neurons. Of these cerebral neurons, only a small number, one to ten percent probably located in the frontal lobe, is conscious at any instant of waking time. The lesser number of frontal lobe neurons must struggle with the problem of a less conscious and subconscious midbrain composed of seventy billion neurons.

The use of words to tell the story of a monotheistic god is an artistic way to improve all too prevalent ineffective human willing and to make it more effective by furnishing ideational subjective support.

From the pragmatic good willing of behaviors to survive, also comes excessively forceful willing known as evil. To attempt to will good and to will less evil, is a pragmatic yet superficial solution to a cosmological and existential problem. To will good and to refrain from evil, is to still possess a changeable will that can express both good and evil behaviors at any time. The goal of existence is not to strengthen and increase human will by imagining a first father companion but to decrease, moderate, and eventually resolve the cosmological function of willing that is resistant to destruction.

A fist father is only subjectively real, and therefore, individuals are not saved by the super willing of a monotheistic companion god. An individual survives life and is saved from oblivion by a subconscious soul of willing for food, sex and reproduction, and aggression. The soul is resistant to destruction as it is a continuation of energy particles of the environment. The only real savior of an individual from the inexorable sequence of life and death, is the conscious self that directs attention to comprehend, discipline, and reduce the default function of the soul to survive. Death cannot destroy the subconscious soul. Conscious willing effort is the only realistic way to moderate subconscious willing function and thereby bring what is resistant to destruction to a gradual ending as a continuation of an evermoving background of a seeming never-ending universe.

Dynamic

The word dynamic is defined as:

"Energy or force that produces motion, objects in movement, interactive systems or functions that consist of competing or conflicting forces of change and progression."

The animating soul is a body and midbrain dynamic of a triune willing for food, sex and reproduction, and aggression. The soul is a continuation of a dynamic system of energy particles of the local environment that is a continuation of a nonlocal dynamic sole cosmological force that exists on its own to ever move the universe.

The soul is a dynamic and dependent continuation that interacts and conflicts with the environment and other living forms through changes of time and repetitive cycles as it repeats to progress. A soul is a real dynamic of midbrain and body while a monotheistic god is an artistic dynamic of story images in the cerebral cortex of the brain. The subjective idea of a first father god saves an individual from worry by providing an optimistic attitude toward life and death. A real animating soul saves as it is a dynamic continuation of a sea of energy particles and is therefore resistant to destruction.

The biblical writers of Genesis used the art of story to communicate that the existential essence of humans is willful disobedience and good and evil knowledge obtained from an ingested fruit, and the evil curses inflicted as punishment by a first father god. In contrast, the modern science of psychology refers to biological instincts and drives as the problematic essence and challenge for an evolved cerebral cortex of the brain.

The God & Soul Theory explains human behavior by utilizing the findings of both religion and science. The theory asserts that there is a conscious self, which is the evolving cerebral cortex of the brain, and a less conscious and subconscious soul which is the midbrain and body functions. The animating and willing soul is a triune dynamic of a hunger for food and water, sex and reproduction, and aggression. The soul is a will-o'-the-wisp dynamic, a web of less conscious and subconscious willing composed of wanting and not wanting. The essential functions of life are a dependent continuation of energy, and must be replenished from the earth and the sun by obtaining food, water, air, and radiation of light and heat. The soul is resistant to destruction as it is a continuation of energy particles of the environment, and a sole cosmological force that continuously moves a universe of dynamic motion.

For monotheistic religions, the mechanism of where life comes from is described in an artistic word portrait story of a first father. The mechanism of saving an individual from destruction of life and death is located outside humans and is said to be a monotheistic god.

However, it is where humans really come from that enables them to survive life and the oblivion of death. Human life has not come from an external first father god but is an internal animating and willing triune soul that is a continuation of real energy elements of the external environment. The human physical body must eventually die but not what animates it from within, a willing soul that can survive death but cannot prevent the body from dying. The soul dynamic is a continuation of energy particles from the external environment, and is an internal function of a triune willing urge of hunger for food and water, sex and reproduction, and aggression that is resistant to destruction.

Reinforcement

A monotheistic god's strong will, reinforces weak human willing to continue despite the struggles of life that progress inevitably to death. Weaker human willing supports its own vulnerable existential function by reinforcing it with subjective artistic stories of a willing first father god. Holding fast to a subjectively imagined first father's strong will, reinforces human willing to live and survive. Humans look past their own faulty willing that makes mistakes, is limited, and is accepted by monotheistic religions to be mortal along with the body that dies. Monotheistic religions do not consider what is inside the body to be important in any way, only what is outside the body is special as the first father origin of existence. This is a grievous mistake, a real bona fide delusion.

Humans overlook and underestimate the importance of their own willing, for the absurd story of a greater external willing of a monotheistic first father who is powerful enough to make the environment and life, and who cares for and protects humans. The real goal of existence is not to imaginatively and artistically reinforce the internal human will to survive with an external first father's will but to reduce human will and to moderate it. Otherwise, anecdotal and case study evidence suggests that as a continuation of a sea of energy particles, human willing resists destruction and continues to survive through life and death.

Humans exist and circumstantial evidence suggests remnant remains of humans continue to exist as a continuation of energy particles of the environment. Souls are a dynamic of habit patterns, of body behaviors, and picture images once formed and located in the cerebral cortex of the brain. Anecdotal and case study evidence suggests that following death, these habit patterns coherently continue to exist.

Company

Human company in a group provides mutual assistance in obtaining work and money, relationships, sexual partners and reproduction, and mutual support and protection from the vicissitudes of life. An imagined monotheistic god provides company so that a person is not alone in life, especially during times of helplessness and hopelessness. The ideation and artistic word story of a first father god is an intellectual resistance to a vulnerable life and death existence.

Faith and belief in the tradition of the word art portrait of a first father god provides additional willing strength to an individual will to better endure life. Humans are happy when they have the help of others. Humans are even happier when they are told and accept that they have the help of a super first father god. Monotheism is the refusal to be alone and is the insistence to be in the company of a first father of many forefathers. The monotheistic group members assist and benefit individual willing, and the subjective idea of a monotheistic god's will, empowers human willing.

It is a false and childish premise to declare that since many previous biological fathers have existed in fact, there must also exist a first father god who made the environment and life. How many otherwise sane individuals have accepted this false premise? How many have died as aggressors and passive martyrs for the subjective word art portrait of a monotheistic god? Countless numbers and many continue to be susceptible and accept the story of a first father who will support and protect them. The subjective idea of a monotheistic god continues to bring comfort and protection to many people, and is often credited with miraculous rescues from harmful situations.

A first father is treated as objectively special when it is only subjectively special. A monotheistic god is a simple superficial story and is not supernatural, it is metaphorical not metaphysical. The subjective idea of an unlimited monotheistic god is a faulty way of reducing a real curse of human limitations. The god is a way of obtaining subjective relief from limitations of human willing and knowledge on the hazardous journey of life and death.

Human company and that of a monotheistic god has its rewards of providing mutual support but excess attention to fellow humans or a first father distract an individual from meditative observation and comprehension of the dynamics of the human self and soul. While the company of a monotheistic god exists only subjectively as a spoken and written word portrait, there does exist a good amount of anecdotal and case study evidence that suggests the objective company of souls.

Error

The cognitive error of accepting subjective word art of a first father god to be objective, is the fault of the conscious cerebral cortex of the brain that strains to make known the unknown origin of existence using a story format. Circa 500 BCE, biblical word artists ideated a monotheistic god and then wrote a word art story as an artistic way of knowing the beginning of existence. Tracing the origin of humans back in time, a leap was made from many good and evil real forefathers to an artistic imagined good first father. The artistic invention of a once-upon-a-time story serves to distract attention from tracing human origin to realistic sexual reproduction and investigation of the supportive environment. This is the real monotheistic origin of sin, of separation.

The Garden of Eden story portrays a real sensed separation, a sin within humans. The story is a lament of separation from an all good beginning in the first chapter of Genesis, to the second and third chapters and a cursed life of good and evil experiences. Life is a curse as what is good does not long endure, and evils too often arrive to linger and worsen.

The metaphorical Genesis story portrays a real internal separation, which is a predominance of lower biological urges of midbrain and body that the higher cerebral cortex has difficulty dealing with. In response, the cerebral cortex spewed forth words to sketch a monotheistic god portrait as a way of reinforcing its psychological functions. The higher cerebral cortex experiences a helplessness as a lower presence within exerts a strong influence from below the limen of conscious awareness. The Garden of Eden story is a metaphor that portrays a real separation of the cerebral cortex brain processes from the midbrain and body functions. The cerebral cortex or conscious self, has separate functions from the midbrain and body dynamic of a less conscious and subconscious soul.

Monotheistic adherents accept that a first father god exists and can help them, especially when it most difficult to help themselves. Human helplessness usually occurs when the environment is nonresponsive to individual needs and desires. Helplessness also occurs within, when the conscious self is dominated by urges from a less conscious and subconscious soul that wants food and water, sex and reproduction, and aggression, and also a plethora of many other things.

Insurance Policy

A monotheistic god resembles an insurance policy that is accepted by many people as a way to be protected during both life and death. The contract policy offered by a monotheistic religion insures that a first father god exists who can protect an individual from risks and unexpected harmful events that occur during life and death. Taught to children and childish adults, a first father god is externalized, utilized, and ritualized into a habit pattern as an internal sanctuary to comfort and protect from harm. The child or adult is taught to appeal to or pray to be protected from harm.

Repeated over time, the subjective idea and behavior becomes an individual habit pattern of imagining and reimagining a monotheistic god as needed.

The subjective artificial habit pattern of seeking refuge is intended to overlay a real innate subconscious habit pattern of a good and evil triune soul, and the external repetitive cycles of environment. The monotheistic ritualized orientation to a first father god is a subjective way to gain freedom from the external repetitive patterns of the environment, and from the internal innate habit patterns and behaviors of the triune soul as a hunger for food, sex and reproduction, and aggression.

What really saves an individual during life and from the oblivion of death, is not a subjective first father god as an idea contained in the cerebral cortex of the brain but the midbrain and body dynamic of a real innate triune soul. Only the cerebral cortex of the human brain contains a first father that functions as a subjective refuge from the external environment and from what animates life internally, a triune soul. The contrived story of a monotheistic god is a way to explain and gain dominance over the physiological dynamic of an animating soul and the physical environment.

Ally

The individual turning of attention to a monotheistic god is oftentimes a response to confusing or desperate situations of life including illness, harm, old age, dying, and death. These experiences prompt the followers of monotheistic religions to ally their own individual willing with the will of a monotheistic god. Individuals may accept the imagined protection of a monotheistic god but the only real protection is that of mutual allied willing of monotheistic group members.

The artistic use of words to portray a monotheistic god is an attempt to elevate the stature of humans from the lowly conditions of life and death. To ally individual willing with the strong willing of a first father is a vicarious way to strengthen one's own will to proceed through and to better survive the hazards of life, ageing, and eventual death. A monotheistic god is a way to support an individual to move forward in life by making it worthwhile and is a way to inspire and uplift a person above the strife and mire of living.

A good, intelligent, and sane first father god is a model to inspire individuals to be good, to use their evolved intelligence to learn, and attempt to remain sane through the crazy experiences of life, replete with many disappointments, desperations, depressions, and dangers.

To entertain the idea of a monotheistic god is a faulty and poor way to have a comprehension of the beginning of existence. To accept a first father god into one's life, is to undergo a conversion to ideational and spoken and written word art, and tradition, and is to commit to a subjective comprehension occurring only in the cerebral cortex of the individual brain. Similar to emotional acceptance of a real beneficent biological father, the experience of accepting an artistically imagined first father triggers personal obedience and an emphasis on ethics of right and wrong and morals. The person who accepts a monotheistic god, also expects assistance to better navigate the uncertainties of life and death.

The good of a first father represents what has been passed down from forefathers, the biological good of sexual pleasure, and needed aggression to protect and to obtain food to survive. The many people who accept the artistic word portrait of a first father, really accept one shared line of biological and ethnic origin. A monotheistic god is a subjective word story of a beginning that represents human biological reproduction that occurs as a continuation of the environment. Instead of perceiving what animates life internally, an external first father god is ideated and supported only by words, faith, trust, and tradition. Individual willing is strengthened with what is accepted to be a good willing first father.

In biblical times, a non-fatherly origin was not known but is now proven to be an unseen willing-like force of energy particles that bring the environment and life into existence. A first father god is an ersatz word model, that serves to make known an unknown origin from what has only recently been verified to exist, real particles of energy. In contrast to the artistic word portrait of a first father animator portrayed in biblical story, an unrecognized triune soul that is a continuation of the supportive energy environment is the real animator of life.

Meditation

Daily life should include some time set aside for meditation, to observe and discipline the conscious self and the less conscious and subconscious soul. Monotheistic religions instruct their followers to essentially ignore internal cognitive processes except to train attention on the internal idea of an external god. The superficial practice of monotheistic rituals usually suffice for much of the population as most lack time to observe and study what occurs in their own brain and body. Falling into the superficial ways of society, with its busy values of family, relationships, and work, leaves none or very little time for observation of internal processes.

There is a failure to observe how conscious sensations endure for only brief seconds, how quickly picture images change, and how conscious willing efforts change to have or be away from. A human subject and an external object are connected via sensations, picture images, and willing for or against. The human body and brain evolved to transform sensations from the senses into picture images of external objects placed in a mental space and arranged into a time sequence of now, past, and future. The resultant content is then commonly referred to as a mind.

Mind is a synonym for mine, for what happens as conscious and subconscious functions inside a physical brain and body. The word mind is a referent, literally "me in or my in" for the internal functions of a physical brain. In daily usage, a referent became a noun and in so doing was added to human vocabulary to confuse as one more unneeded psycho-babble term.

In popular parlance, the human mind is then said to have thoughts. The English word thought, means an object appears in a space of human conscious attention, and in time meaning tied to the object in a sequence of now sensations, and now, past, or future picture images. Thinking is to have object images appear in subjective conscious attention. If the images are indistinct, they are generally called thoughts.

A thought is a thou, an external person or object also located as an internal picture image perceived within a thee or subject, in a dynamic space and time sequence of change. The English suffix *ght* forms words such as thought, light, might, fight, right, night, flight, height, and a few hundred more. This suffix seems to have been reversed through time to *thg* and eventually changed to stand on its own as *the*. The word thought can then be comprehended to mean the thou, meaning an external object in an internal thee or subject.

Meditation is a practice of training conscious attention to better focus and to observe and comprehend internal processes of brain and body. During meditation, there must be a moderation of excess attention to sensations, and a training of attention to moderate excess picture images of now, past, and future. Meditation is the training to focus attention to reduce willing for sensations of objects, and for picture images of objects in space and time. If something occupies a space, it of necessity occupies a time sequence of change having a beginning and ending. The individual subject is in time, tied to an object via sensations, picture images, and willing. The meditator trains the brain to moderate willing for sensations of seeing, hearing, smelling, tasting, and touching of an object by not placing it in a space and time sequence picture image of now, past, or future. The willing for an object places it in a space and a time sequence. This occurs as a subconscious perception that may or may not become less conscious and progress to conscious.

It is a benefit to practice meditation, to focus attention and cultivate moderation so as not to excessively will for sensations of seeing, hearing, smelling, tasting, and touching of external objects. It is beneficial to not overly will for picture images of now, past, and future. It is a benefit to not excessively will for or against any internal picture image of an external object. Observing that sensations only briefly endure from second to second, it is not worthwhile to overly will for them. Observing picture images are fleeting, it is not worth overly willing for them. The individual trains conscious attention to let go of and not to excessively will for picture images of now, past, or future.

What is worthwhile is to moderate willing so as to better see clearly and to not overly will for or against. This practice calms the internal mechanism of picture images and especially of excessive willing for food, sex and reproduction, and aggression. Not practicing meditation, background sensations of noise, of comings and goings of human activity, contribute to a subconscious effort of wanting to continue to take part in ongoing events. There is a wanting to go on and wanting to avoid an end or oblivion. There is no cultivation of stillness, of not going and a discipline of not wanting to go on. Therefore, the triune soul continues to exist.

Meditative observation and investigation unglues and pulls apart the agglutination, the knotted mass of conscious and subconscious sensations, picture images, and willing. Consistent practice of meditation releases the strands of bondage of the inner with outer reality. Exhilaration spontaneously occurs, and promotes clear comprehension, relative peace and calm. For the person who meditatively moderates willing for sensations of the senses, willing for picture images of now, past, and future, and calms excess willing for or against, the world comes to an end and continues not.

Clarity

For the great majority of humans, there is a lack of clarity and instead only a muddled comprehension of life and death. During the practice of training attention through meditation, an individual must slog through a dense fog of inattention and distraction, until following consistent efforts, a phenomenal clear space may at some time appear. This phenomenon is a dynamic clarity of focused attention. Phenomenal clarity cannot be reached by most, as attention is distracted by contents of the conscious self (cerebral cortex) of sensations and picture images, and the subconscious soul (midbrain and body) of willing urges of hunger for food, sex and reproduction, and aggression. Through the consistent practice of meditation, existing only briefly at first, then gradually lengthening in duration, there develops a lessening of attention to sensations, picture images, and willing.

It is then, reduced to little or lacking objects of attention, that a subjective space of clarity opens. The clarity was not previously existent as attention was distracted but when attention is bereft of its usual phenomenal contents, then spontaneously appears clarity and a space of refuge.

When a meditating individual slowly disciplines attention not to place objects in a space and to stay in now time, there ceases a cluttering of objects within the individual conscious subject. The individual must empty much of the objects of attention, and in so doing a clear space opens within. Reducing object content of the conscious self and reducing subconscious urges of the soul is difficult, yet with consistent practice of training attention, the individual is made to be without object content and a subjective clarity ensues of a phenomenal space.

Subject

The English word subject is derived from Latin (prefix *sub*, below or under, and *iacere*, to throw). There exists within a person an internal subject that throws out images of objects from below or under, and from a place where the process cannot be observed. There exists a phenomenal human subject composed of a subconscious soul and a conscious self. For much of human existence, the subconscious soul has not been recognized or only poorly and popularly defined. The soul is subconscious and primary and it throws out willing urges for food and water, sex and reproduction, and aggression to better survive life. The conscious self directs or throws out attention to sensations and from these makes picture images of now, past, and future that stimulate willing behaviors.

There also exists a noumenal subject that exists on its own and cannot be observed by humans as it ejects, throws out objects of the environment from the unobserved depths of seemingly infinite space and time, and the earth throws out living forms. In monotheistic religions this continuation of subjects is primitively made known and falsely connoted by the word portrait story of a first father god.

Meditative Attention

A meditation discipline must train attention to observe and not ignore the dynamic of the human self and soul. Consistent meditative effort of focusing attention, leads to comprehension and clarity, and with a trained ability to focus there can be noticed and observed a second by second change of sensations of seeing, hearing, smelling, tasting, and touching of either pleasure or pain. A trained focus of attention can better observe a rapid change of picture images of now, past, and future. A focus of attention is needed to observe that conscious willing is changeable while subconscious willing efforts of the cell and organ functions of the body last longer in comparison.

It requires time and consistent effort to train attention and to develop the ability to focus and to clearly distinguish the internal dynamic trio of sensations, picture images, and willing efforts. Immediate objects exist outside of the body, which excite sensations inside as seeing hearing, smelling, tasting, and touching. From sensations are made picture images of objects to exist in a space and time sequence. Supported by this dynamic, conscious willing exerts effort for or against as a continuation of a subconscious willing dynamic of the triune soul of hunger for food and water, sex and reproduction, and aggression.

External objects can be noticed or ignored. The same with internal psychological functions as sensations of seeing, hearing, smelling, tasting, and touching that are either pleasurable or painful. Picture images of now, past, or future consist of external objects placed in an internal space and time sequence. This activates a conscious willing for or against that is not long lasting but can be made to be longer lasting by repetition to form less conscious and subconscious habit patterns of behavior.

A meditative focus of attention can observe conscious willing effort to be a continuation of subconscious willing effort of cell and organ function, and life to be a continuation of the earth and sun environment.

The conglomerate of continuous changing conscious sensations, picture images of external objects placed in an internal space and time sequence, and conscious and less conscious willing effort is a trio dynamic of the subconscious triune soul as it wills for food and water, sex and reproduction, and aggression. Through a meditative focus of attention, sensations can be observed to continuously change from second to second. Observing this phenomenon of sensate change, picture images of external objects placed in internal space and time sequence, and conscious willing effort may gradually disengage, and are temporarily reduced or held in abeyance. Observing picture images of now experience, memory, or images of future to be rapidly changing, there occurs a temporary release of them.

Meditatively observing continuous change of sensations and picture images of now, past, and future, lessens attention for conscious willing effort to want what comes and goes so quickly and endures for only moments. Like scintillating sparks, sensations do not long endure. The meditator reduces attention to sensations and refrains from making picture images from them of now, past, and future. Conscious willing changes, wills now for this and then for that object. Subconscious willing is less changeable as willing efforts are the habitual functions of cells and organs of the body.

Seeing the time sequence of sensations of seeing, hearing, smelling, tasting, and touching do not long endure and last but for seconds, while pragmatically useful, are not so valuable. The meditator reduces the forming of picture images from the sensations that last but briefly, reduces willing for the fleeting sensations and picture images, and adjusts conscious willing to balance in situations of for and against.

Enlightenment

For the average nonmeditating person, sensations, picture images, and conscious and subconscious willing are blurred and not distinct from each other. Early Hindus and Buddhists developed preternatural methods of meditation by focusing conscious attention to look steadily inward and to observe brain and body functions.

It was observed by them that too much attention was directed to sensations, so meditation was practiced with eyes closed in a quiet place. Meditators surely observed a stream of picture images of now, past, and future, and so reduced attention to and calmed them. Sensations change from second to second, and picture images of now, past, and future last only briefly.

The meditator must have observed the functions of conscious, less conscious, and subconscious willing. Conscious willing is changeable from moment to moment, such as to move the body, sit, stand, or walk. Conscious and subconscious willing, forms habit patterns that are long-lasting, resistant to change, and tend to repeat. To train attention to observe and comprehend these phenomenal processes is what is meant by enlightenment. In toto, the individual must train to focus conscious attention, and to distinguish, and illuminate the dynamic phenomena of the self and soul with the light of personal comprehension.

A few individuals but not many, make the willing effort to meditatively observe and to comprehend a human self and soul. It requires time and effort to direct attention to comprehend the conscious self and to moderate or resolve subconscious habit patterns of the soul. Individual effort is required to observe there is conscious willing and picture images, as well as subconscious willing urges and dream images of the midbrain and body.

The ersatz substitute for self and soul observation and exploration, is an artistic word portrait that brings comfort to many people who cannot manage to look inward but instead direct attention outward to a monotheistic god. Most busy people prefer an external god to protect them rather than to rely on internal effort to resolve problems or to learn about the self and soul. Unlike Hindus and Buddhists who developed methods of meditation, the founders and followers of monotheistic religions focused attention on the ideational word portrait of a greater first father god. Middle East monotheistic religions promote faith, belief, and the tradition of a first father god via the spoken and written word art of scriptures.

Humans need help with life, especially with their individual willing. Rather than enlightened observation of the self and soul, monotheistic religions accept a vague and dim artistic word portrait of a first father, a subjective story character brought into existence sketched with verbal and written words.

Survival

Case study reports of near-death experiences, childhood reincarnation memories, after-death visits by deceased relatives and friends, and many sightings and sensing of ghosts, suggest but do not prove that there is a real dimension the human soul transits to after death. If there is a real near-earth dimension of an afterlife, it is necessary to better comprehend the soul and where its roots of growth and life come from and may transit to.

For humans there are two kinds of willing, conscious and subconscious. Conscious willing occurs in the cerebral cortex and central nervous system, while less conscious and subconscious willing occurs in the midbrain and body and autonomic nervous system. A soul is a subconscious willing habit pattern grounded in energy particles. The essence of human survival is an animating soul of habit patterns of willing behaviors bonded with some conserved conscious picture images. The soul is a continuation of and is bonded with the willing-like energy particles of the changing earth and sun environment.

The best estimate of modern neuroscience, is that the human brain consists of eighty-six billion neurons. Of this number, only sixteen billion or roughly fourteen percent of total neurons make up the cerebral cortex and are capable of conscious reasoning and imagining. The other seventy billion and eighty-six percent of brain neurons have less conscious and subconscious functions of the autonomic nervous system. Of the fourteen percent of neurons that make up the cerebral cortex of the brain, only a small percentage located in the frontal lobe, estimated to be from one to ten percent, is conscious at any point of waking time.

The brain percentages support the assertion that the less conscious and subconscious soul is superior to the conscious capable self, at least in terms of neuron dominance. Anecdotal and case study evidence suggests that something may survive death of the body and supported by the findings of neuroscience, probably also consists of an approximate ratio of fourteen percent conscious and eighty-six percent less conscious and subconscious.

The conscious self is usually fearful of dying, and wants to save its ability to have picture images or to think after death. It can do so only as it is a relative evolved function of the dominant less conscious and subconscious soul. Following death, the conscious self continues to be faced with the unfinished tasks of life, especially to better comprehend what animates it, the less conscious and subconscious animating and willing triune soul.

The only way to remove the renowned metaphorical Christian sin of separation of lower behaved humans from a higher first father god, is to practice meditative observation of a real separation. The real human separation is of a lower midbrain and body from an evolved higher cerebral cortex of the brain. Meditative attention must observe the conscious self and second by second change of sensations, and the continuing change of conscious picture images.

The individual must also observe the less conscious demanding midbrain and body soul urges of hunger for food and water, sex and reproduction, and aggression. This is the way the primordial separation can be healed, by attention and guidance by the conscious self to discipline and direct the less conscious and subconscious triune soul to what is better and best in life.

Wrestling

Existence is a struggle of wrestling with personal illness, injury, the environment, other life forms, family members, coworkers, fellow humans, and internal functions of individual brain and body, and with words.

In response to wrestling with the external environment and with the internal animating soul, and often losing, followers of monotheistic religions accept the subjective sheltering story, the word art portrait of a protective first father god. Having the idea of a monotheistic god can then subjectively and temporarily elevate those who accept the tale, above the fray of daily life, wrestling with conditions of the external environment, other humans, and with an internal hunger for food and water, sex and reproduction, and aggression. If the wrestling match of life is not won and resolved, anecdotal and case study evidence suggests the struggle will continue after death.

Continuation of the soul may be similar to when the brain and body sleep, the less conscious and subconscious soul continues to animate life functions. After death, the soul also continues its saving, animating, and willing function, and as anecdotal reports and case studies of childhood reincarnation memories often convincingly suggest, can recur. As a continuation of a sea of energy particles of the environment, the soul is resistant to destruction and continues to animate and to reanimate.

The ability to resurrect attributed to a monotheistic god is an ability thieved from the animating soul that can reanimate by developing in the reproductive cycle of a living female body. For those wrapped in a monotheistic diaper and the security blanket of a first father god, this may seem strange indeed. But so is quantum theory strange to all who hear it explained and just as difficult to fully comprehend.

Retreat

Retreating to a quiet environment, an individual can reduce distracting and stressful effects of society for a short or longer time. The word retreat is defined as:

"A behavior of withdrawing, moving back or away from something harmful. A time or place of peace, quiet, privacy, seclusion, retirement, and solitude, for the intention of study, meditation or prayer."

A retreat can contribute multiple physical and psychological benefits including:

- Provide a simplified structure of daily routine to remove profane and frivolous distractions of daily life
- Provide quiet time for meditation
- Provide leisure for study and an increase of comprehension and clarity of knowledge and wisdom
- Reduce willful conflict with fellow humans

To accomplish an increase of cognitive clarity, the retreatant must be free from the general population of the disinterested and distracted. Some retreatants practice silence by observing a vow to not speak for variable days of time. Not speaking facilitates less distraction and more time to observe brain and body functions. A vow of silence enables a better contemplative focus of attention that may illuminate an answer intentionally or unintentionally sought to a question, problem, or situation.

Retreatants with a monotheistic orientation will focus on a first father as a higher good and pray to receive guidance from the god. Monotheistic monks and mystics attempt to reach an increase of comprehension and higher level of intelligence and knowledge through a personal revelation from a first father god. What they are actually seeking is better comprehension of their own cerebral cortex of the brain and body. An answer to a question is intuitively or psychically revealed by the cerebral cortex of the brain but often falsely attributed to a monotheistic god.

What a retreatant seeks is cognitive clarity of the conscious cerebral cortex of the brain, which is what a monotheistic god represents and is where it subjectively exists as an idea and a word story, and nowhere else. A monotheistic god represents a way of obtaining personal freedom from conscience of painful picture images of past and ongoing wrongs. Dependent personality types beg a first father to relieve them of poignant feelings of guilt and confusion but these heartfelt petitions are in vain.

Tears of repentance are undoubtedly therapeutic. However, like rituals of baptism, immersion, or sprinkling of blessed water, seeking forgiveness from a monotheistic god is a vain subjective attempt to wash away objective memories of past and ongoing regrets and wrongs.

Non-monotheistic individuals, such as Buddhists and Taoists, do not need an ideational first father god. They are content with cultivating individual comprehension. This can be accomplished by training attention to meditatively observe and learn about the higher functions of the cerebral cortex and the lower functions of midbrain and body. A non-monotheistic retreat is an effort and opportunity to improve clarity of comprehension, improve ethics and morals, and is a pragmatic effort to seek relief from conscience and deeds done in the past.

A retreatant may gain better comprehension of the less conscious and subconscious functions of midbrain and body dynamic of a triune soul as a hunger for food, sex and reproduction, and aggression. An individual may benefit from a retreat by an increase of creativity, intuition, psychic perception, and and perhaps waking or dream guidance from deceased relatives and friends.

Certainly, an aspiring individual will encounter difficulty with boredom and sleep while weening attention away from distracting sensations and picture images in the conscious cerebral cortex. The conscious self will also wrestle to comprehend and discipline the subconscious demands of midbrain and body dynamic of the triune soul.

Poise

Rather than look within the human body and brain as an effective way to solve the problems of life, the founders of monotheistic religion looked outside, and with use of a word portrait of story identified a first father god who could help humans with the problems of life and death.

Instead of observing and acquiring knowledge, and solving the challenges caused by a real animating soul and environment, monotheism opted for the subjective word story of a fatherly god. A poignant problem of humankind is that there exists only a subjective monotheistic first father. In contrast, there exists a real objective environment, and as a continuation of it, a real animating triune soul as a hunger for food and water, sex and reproduction, and aggression. In the metaphorical Genesis story, the first humans willfully disobeyed and separated themselves from the authoritative willing of a first father god. This is the Christian egregious myth of sin, the origin of separation from goodness.

To comprehend the metaphor, it must be interpreted correctly, not using theological terminology but rather with use of physiological and psychological terms. The monotheistic artistic myth of a first father god is a way of saying the higher willing and knowing conscious functions of the cerebral cortex of the brain conflict with the subconscious lower midbrain and body dynamic of a triune soul.

In legend, the good Buddha encountered the evil Mara, who encouraged him to live life and perform traditional rituals as a refuge and to give up his struggle for clearer comprehension of life and death. (Sutta Nipata) The mythic tale of Jesus tells of his encounter with a Devil who tempted him with lower values and goals in an attempt to prevent him from reaching a higher comprehension. (Luke 4:1-14) The word devil is a noun version of the verb evil. The evil of excessive force exists in the external geological and meteorological events of the environment, and as a continuation of it, also within humans as an animating and willing triune soul.

The main problem of human life is a lack of knowledge of the animating and dynamic essence of a triune soul. The soul often indulges inordinately in willing for food, sex and reproduction, and aggression. Over indulging in food leads to poor health, while indulging in sex leads to jealousy, possessiveness, reproduction and a family and the toil of life to provide care and protection. Indulging in aggression often leads to injury and death.

Conscious attention can train, reduce, and moderate behaviors. There must be an increase or a decrease of willing, an adjusting of balance to not under or over eat food, have sex and reproduction, and express aggression. Many people lack an ability to adjust and balance, and instead live maladjusted and unbalanced lives.

The conscious human self is an evolute of a less conscious and subconscious soul that is a continuation of a non-conscious environment. Only the human conscious self can do the work to balance the less conscious and subconscious triune soul, the dynamic of which is a hunger for food, sex and reproduction, and aggression. A monotheistic god who intervenes in human life, is only subjectively helpful to those who accept the first father artistic word portrait.

The culture of India developed pragmatic means to adjust the self and soul functions, such as the practice of yoga dating from circa 3,200 BCE, and utilized since then to discipline willing of the body to maintain health, and to balance eating of food, sex and reproduction, and aggression. Yoga postures balance subconscious willing of midbrain and body and conscious willing of the cerebral cortex of the brain. India's renowned son Buddha, further developed meditation par excellence to more closely observe and discipline individual willing and thereby reduce reincarnation through many lives. To accomplish this, he developed the practice of retirement to forest living, eating one meal daily, no sex or reproduction, and compassion to reduce aggression.

The rare wonder of personal poise is the moderating Middle Way of Buddha, and the virtue of the midpoint between the extremes of excess and deficit in the Golden Mean of Aristotle. Moderation is emphasized in one of two inscriptions over the oracular temple of Apollo at Delphi (Greek, *meden agan*) translated as "nothing excess." A balance of the self and soul made habitual is the natural peace of Nirvana, and may be the peace mentioned that surpasses the understanding of many. (Philippians 4:7)

Breath of Life

Having no method and no obvious interest in observing what now animates life within the body, monotheistic word artist scribes instead focused attention on what did animate life in the past and from outside, a first father that represents generations of forefathers. Monotheistic male word-artist writers made up a his-story of male precedence in a once-upon-a-time genealogy.

In the biblical Garden of Eden story, the animating essence of life is portrayed as a breath from the first father god to the first human. (Genesis 2:7) This is a unique moment as a special animating will to live and move was placed inside of humans. For monotheistic theology, when the body dies the breath ceases as does human free will and both are then not regarded as special, they are just ordinary functions of a physical body.

The metaphorical animating breath of the first father god is special as it is the animating and willing of life, yet once inside and when the body dies, it is suddenly not special and is only a physical and mundane function. In the Genesis story, attention is focused on the only animator, the monotheistic god and not on the special transmitted animation from the first father to the first human. Following death, breathing stops and the body no longer freely and willingly moves and can only be resurrected by the monotheistic god. The breath, alias the much-touted free will, is dissipated at the time of death until eventually restored to the resurrected body of helpless humans by the first father. For monotheistic religions, the only importance for humans is the body containing a breath and free will that are all to be resurrected.

The breath of life portrayed as coming from the metaphorical first father, is more than simple breathing; it is a special transfer of free will to humans, so they can willingly and freely move about and live. The first father is an artistic story character that only metaphorically and poorly explains how human life is animated and wills to live. The real animating essence is not an external monotheistic god who animates human life but is a real internal soul that is a continuation of the external metaphysical energy particles of the environment.

Words

Monotheistic religions often refer to writings about a first father as the "word of god." The words about a monotheistic god are really those of human authors used to identify the cultural origin and to bestow a level of authority and superiority upon themselves. The way monotheistic religions identify the origin of existence is not objective, measurable, or experimental but consists of spoken and written word artistry. A monotheistic god is a primitive good, ideated by the cerebral cortex of the brain for the good of knowing the beginning of existence and of having subjective protection. The subjective idea of a monotheistic first father god is the cognitive good of how the cerebral cortex identifies its own origin deemed to be an overall good for humankind.

A monotheistic god story is an artistic achievement of word art by the cerebral cortex of the brain. Accepting the artistic word portrait of a first father provides only subjective assurance to an individual that they are protected and can live without worry on a dangerous earth. This is as children do who experience protection when under the gaze of their real biological earthly father. The reality of a series of previous biological fathers cannot be sanely extended and extrapolated to the subjective idea and artistic story of a first father. Yet monotheistic sacerdotalists offer the supportive stratagem of a word portrait first father to the needy for a donation of money to support their own livelihood. The idea of a monotheistic god is a subjective benefit to humans but to imagine it to be objective crosses the line from sane to insane.

Not an objective interactive first father but a subjective idea and words in the cerebral cortex of the brain helps many humans allay worry, fear, and the sad times of daily life. A monotheistic god also helps many to have subjective control of the external environment and the internal dynamic urges of hunger for food, sex and reproduction, and aggression. The word portrait of a monotheistic god is deemed an acceptable fib offered by sacerdotalists and welcomed by many as a way to feel better about life and death.

Order

Chapter 1 of the biblical Genesis story portrays the monotheistic god bringing the orderly environment and life into existence. In the chapters that follow, the first humans were blamed for their willing sin of disobedience and disorder. They were punished to live outside of the paradise garden on the semi-orderly good and evil earth, separate from interaction with and shunned by the god. During orderly times a first father is thanked, and during times of disorder the god represents where to turn attention and appeal or pray to for order. The monotheistic god is orderly, made order and can impose order sometimes, and is therefore a refuge from disorder. Some greater order is needed to impose relative order on the disorder that the environment and life consists of including weather, accident, illness, aggression, the disorder of ageing, and the decaying disorder of death.

Who to turn to but to the maker of order, yet if the first father has not made disorder, he at least allows it to exist and flourish. It is the business of evangelists and sacerdotalists to arouse individuals to accept on faith and tradition a first father beginning of existence, and to persuade them to an orderly ethical and moral life. Monotheistic sacerdotalists see their paid role in life, to reduce and relieve the effect of curses received by the first humans from the first father god in the Garden of Eden story. The first father curse it seems, has been incurred by later humans, and is daily observed not to be lifted through the passing years by a subjective and therefore ineffective monotheistic god. There is no objective metaphysical omnipotent god, there exists only a subjective metaphorical impotent word art portrait of a first father.

Just as in the Garden of Eden story, so too in human relationships, everything looks very good in the beginning stages. It is only a matter of time and of looking more closely at a person that the not so good of the other individual is seen, as well as the foibles and glaring failings of the evolved human condition. A contest of wills sooner or later erupts despite even the best of intentions to love and honor each other.

Orderly intimate relationships and friendships are based only on what can be comfortably tolerated in the other person, otherwise there develops the disorder of disagreement and conflict. The disorder of life, of being preyed upon and recognizing the tendency within to prey upon others, leads many people to accept a monotheistic god as a way to insure an orderly life.

Since the first father is in perpetual absentia and never intervenes to reduce disorder or restore order, in all cultures exist strong charismatic leaders who form armies to defend the society and to conquer other rulers who threaten order with the aggression and disorder of war. No unearthly ruler, only earthly rulers form governments and the legal system of laws and rules to direct individual willing and to maintain social order.

Order and Disorder

Life consists of both order and disorder, and more than a few humans on the earth seek order for their lives by appealing to where many accept that order first came from, a monotheistic god. Observing the universe, there exists overall order yet disorder abounds as isolated collisions of galaxies, stars, planets, comets, and asteroids as they collide and explode releasing energy. There is also daily and nightly order and disorder of conflict among living forms from the smallest to the largest.

In the Judaic Middle East, the effort to comprehend the order and disorder of existence was the artistic response of story about a first father god. A monotheistic god is a human pretense of knowledge of where the order and disorder of existence comes from. There was no sensible effort to comprehend order and disorder as did the inquiring observational Greek and Hindu cultures. Monotheistic religions accept a first father to exist who has an ultra-willing and knowing ability with which the god made the environment and life. But the willing and knowing by a monotheistic god is flawed by being capable of both good and evil, a trait the god also shares with humans he made to exist.

Since the god's will is free and capable of willing both good and evil, humans have the identical trait. In the Genesis story, the disorder of human life is traced to the free will placed into them by the first father god. Human free will can do or not do, obey or not obey, and this ability brought about the sinister disorder of willing good and evil.

The god further willed some of his good and evil knowledge into a tree and its fruit. Having a free will, humans freely acquired the arboreal knowledge and proceeded to use it to will the good of order and the evil of disorder. A serious *fait accompli*. A real explanation is that humans do contribute to the disorder of life by a lack of knowledge and by conscious willing that is directed by the less conscious and subconscious willing of an animating soul of hunger for food and water, sex and reproduction, and aggression.

In the monotheistic myth of Genesis, the god represents order while the first humans represent the disorder of life. Humans are portrayed as guilty of causing the disorder of life that is later pronounced by Christians to be an original sin of separation from the orderly good of the god. Many members of monotheistic religions accept there is a separation from the good of a first father god. They look to be rejoined with, to bask in the presence of, and to be favored by the god. The theological story is, someday after the disorder of death occurs, the monotheistic god will reorder and resurrect the breath, the free will, and the body. *Viola*.

Lacking good and reliable human relationships, it is easy enough to ideate the company of a first father and god. Sacerdotalists encourage individuals to divert their attention in this way, away from troubles and problems to the idea of a first father. Attending the worship service of a monotheistic god is to at least take part in the outer semblance of order and hope for restoration of inner order by dispelling disorders such as worry, stress, illness, and conflict of relationships. Order and disorder are imagined to be observed by an onlooking first father god who imposes order and can punish intentional human disorder. An orderly social or religious gathering is preferred by all attendees.

In the Genesis story, the god used voice commands to bring the orderly environment and life into existence. Later throughout the Tanak, the first father gave as many as 613 voice commandments to enforce social order. In the story, the god represents the cerebral cortex of the brain that rules the less intelligent midbrain and body and the nonintelligent order and disorder of the environment. The god represents the order of the reasoning cerebral cortex of the brain, while the role of the first humans represent the disorder of the midbrain and body functions and the hunger for food and water, sex and reproduction, and aggression.

Each individual must responsibly cultivate the order of health through diet and exercise. Order of midbrain and body is accomplished by discipline of hunger for food, sex and reproduction, and aggression. Knowledge reduces the disorder of ignorance. Consistent meditation brings order and a better focus of attention and reduces the disorder of sensory distractions. Meditation practice brings about a focus of attention and order to the cerebral cortex of the brain. Work and financial security reduce the disorder of poverty and limitation. Supportive relationships contribute to order of family, friends, and coworkers, and reduces disorder of conflict, loneliness, and lack of support.

All becomes disordered through time but there is a saving suborder of energy particles that saves individual subconscious habit patterns of behaviors and picture images. It is as a continuation of particle energy, and a life of willing behavior patterns and picture images that causes coherence of the soul and is resistant to destruction. Entering the dimension of death, no first father waits there to insure an orderly passage. When behavior and picture image patterns that are the soul encounter the volume of fine circular particles of energy, there is a tendency for coherence and perhaps as anecdotal and case studies suggest, an orderly circulation from the afterlife dimension to earth again.

Lower to Higher

The tradition of psycho-active plant and drug inebriation is a way of reducing inner limitation and getting to a higher pleasure and away from what is lower, mundane, and painful. The down side is that drug use has to be repeated as the body and brain habituate so that the experience of the induced high and painlessness lessens over time. A traditional way to separate from what is lower is to do what is higher or good. To do good gives an uplifting feeling following the deed. Philosophies, religions, psychology, and governments provide theories of ethics and laws to guide individuals to what is good. The monotheistic word portrait of a first father is also a primitive way of directing attention to what is higher and thereby serves to distance an individual from so much of what is lower on the earth.

Purported knowledge of a monotheistic god is not objective knowledge but is subjective. Sometime in the not too distant future, more humans will reach a higher level of comprehension that a first father god is a subjective artistic and lower work of word art. Humans will also soon reach a higher comprehension that the soul is a triune dynamic of hunger for food and water, sex and reproduction, and aggression, and as a continuation of energy particles of the environment is resistant to destruction.

Pleasure

Life consists of pleasure and pain experiences. The ideational pleasure artistically expressed in the word portrait of a monotheistic god is subjectively intended to temporarily reduce and remove attention from the many displeasures of existence. Individual willing that is supported by a greater willing, enables vulnerable humans to proceed in life amid many dangers and inevitable ageing and death. Since the willing of family members, friends, and fellow humans, cannot always be relied upon, nor is the willing-like change of the environment always beneficial, the greater willing of a first father assists human willing to be safe and more successful. Attention to a monotheistic god temporarily reduces attention to human limitations. The ideated, spoken, and written word portrait of a willing first father subjectively reduces the limitations of adherents and vicariously expands human limits of conscious willing.

A first father god is an artistic way out of human limitations imposed by the environment and the evolved limits of human willing and knowing. A monotheistic god is a refusal to accept the limitation of not knowing the origin of existence, and a refusal to be overly limited by harmful situations of life experience. Accepting a monotheistic god, humans can then appeal to an unlimited maker of the environment and life. Unfortunately, a monotheistic god is an artistic conception and word portrait fiction and not a reality perception.

Those who advocate for and seek to persuade others about the existence of a monotheistic god, insist that humans must look to and accept the pleasurable idea and word portrait of a first father as a way to reduce the many displeasures of life and death. Monotheistic religions suggest that an individual must focus attention and have faith and belief that the greatest pleasure of life exists beyond the many small pleasures of a brief lifetime. The ideational pleasure of a long-lasting monotheistic god is preferred while the brief pleasures of food, sex, and aggression quickly fade into nonexistence and often disappointment.

A monotheistic god is a focus of attention to an ideational pleasure and away from the many real displeasures of life and death. A first father is a pinpoint of pleasure sustained only by faith, belief, and tradition, a way of knowing the origin of existence rather than the poignant displeasure of not knowing how the environment and life began.

For many people, the pleasurable belief in the existence of a first father god provides relief by subjectively overriding the often-bleak reality of rapidly changing smaller pleasures of life. A monotheistic god is an ideational pleasure that protects from displeasures. A story of a first father god is word art intended to be utilized to distract attention from existence. A monotheistic god represents the false claim of superiority by the conscious cerebral cortex of the human brain as it subjectively and artistically directs attention away from a real and often confusing environment and conflicting human behaviors.

The idea of a monotheistic god represents superiority of the conscious cerebral cortex of the brain as it imagines a way to explain and control the less conscious and subconscious willing functions of the midbrain and body dynamic of a triune soul.

Life consists of the goal of going from one pleasure to another and of avoiding pains. Looking for small pleasures is like searching for and finding wildflowers to pick and enjoy for a short time. Their existence can be prolonged but briefly by placing them in a vase of water, until the attractive petals soon wilt and the sweet odor fades. Once pleasurable, they are fit only to be thrown away without much sadness, with only a lingering wistfulness for small pleasures that were but are no longer.

Garden of Eden

In the Garden of Eden story, the monotheistic god formed every beast and bird of the air from the ground (Genesis 2:19) but the story does not mention that the god breathed a breath of life into them. It is mentioned that the first father made the first human body from the red soil of the earth and breathed a breath and a free will movement of life into the first human. (Genesis 2:7) The Genesis story tells that the first father banished the first humans from the paradise Garden of Eden (Genesis 3:24) and since then, humans toil for food, have sex and reproduce, and exert aggression. Though not mentioned in the story, based on observation, so too all of life on the earth must have been banished as microorganisms, plants, and animals continue to struggle day and night to aggressively consume each other to live and reproduce.

Innate within the cells and organs of life, exists the potential for both good and evil, function and dysfunction. The family tree of life is sustained by the good and evil dynamic of hunger for food and water, sex and reproduction, and competitive aggression. Life is rooted in the energy particles of the supportive earth below and the sun environment above. Life is only subjectively rooted in an artistic word portrait story of a monotheistic god.

Rather than a real growth from the earth, in monotheistic religions life is portrayed in story as coming from the character of a first father god. Life is a real dynamic rooted in and growing from the earth but is occluded with the simplistic story of a monotheistic god who acts only on the stage of subjective human imagination. Stories are for entertainment and monotheistic theological stories of a first father is intended to entertain and thereby distract individuals from facing the real dramas and traumas of life and death.

The roots of life do not extend to a first father god imagined by the conscious cerebral cortex of a monotheistic brain but is an internal animating soul that is rooted in and is a continuation of the environment. The roots of experience are in waking conscious attention that consists of sensations and picture images of now, past, and future, while what is less conscious and subconscious consists of cellular function that is a continuation of the environment. Coming from and supported by the ground of the environment grows and goes the willing behaviors of life. The dynamic of growth occurs within each individual cell of human brain and body. Hunger for food and water, sex and reproduction, and aggression are a triune function within the cells of life. This process is a continuation of and is rooted in and is supported by the bodies of earth and sun environment, and the metaphysical energy particles of which they are composed.

Buddha

The two cultures of India and the Orient developed methods of meditation to better observe the dynamic of life and the environment. Meditation focuses attention and lessens distractions that in turn lead to better comprehension, reliable experiential knowledge, and mental hygiene.

Founders of religions do the difficult work of searching for the origin of existence and communicating what they discover to others. Siddhartha Gautama (circa 623-543 BCE) later known as Buddha, sought to better comprehend the functions of the conscious self and the less conscious and subconscious soul.

How thankful many must be that he accepted the existential challenge and made the effort to awaken and comprehend life and death. Not at all an easy task. There surely must have been a long precursor of effort (hence extant legends) to have such an interest in self and soul exploration. Who would even set as their goal in life, to want to struggle toward such a difficult task to better comprehension of the conscious self and the less conscious and subconscious soul dynamic? Why even bother to make the effort to comprehend the internal dynamics of self and soul, and to make known what for most will surely remain unknown?

If Buddha had not exerted effort to comprehend life and death, he would have lived an average life, would have gained weight from over-eating, would have had kids and a wife to toil for and support by earning a princely living. He would have expressed aggression and suffered insult, injury, and death from enemies. Life would have been busy and non-notable, with little available time to better comprehend existence.

In contrast to the successful efforts of Buddha, the good intentioned but misguided founders of monotheistic religions and their later minions, failed to explore the human self and soul. Instead, they struggled to find the origin of existence and finally subjectively identified it to be a first father god. The idea continues to be generated and bolstered by belief and tradition. The artistic idea and word art of a good first father is a simplistic way to identify the origin of existence, and following the god's paternal commandments lead to a partial good of social order. The monotheistic mythic message is to take refuge in what is elevated, the subjective word art portrait of a first father god generated by the higher cerebral cortex of the human brain.

Good and Evil Fruit

Back in the day, Genesis writers subjectively ideated a monotheistic god in the cerebral cortex of the brain. Over time, the idea was portrayed in a word portrait of story.

The spoken and written story masquerades as the origin of existence, and is offered to the uncritical and gullible as objective and reliable knowledge. Why continue to perpetuate this theological hoax on humankind? The probable answer is that the purveyed idea of a first father god yields the pleasant fruits of identifying the unknown origin of existence, and also provides subjective care and protection to those in need.

The artistic scribes who imagined the idea and portrayed the story knowledge of a monotheistic god undoubtedly utilized the word art portrait to obtain positions of authority in the culture, and the ploy continues to be used today for the same purpose. For humankind, the story knowledge of a monotheistic god is like all things, both good and evil. The idea of a first father is only good as it defines an unknown origin and provides subjective protection. The evil is that the subjective idea and artistic word portrait of a monotheistic god is falsely portrayed as objective. The delusion then offered and accepted by many people gives only a false and harmful help and hope. While humans as a species have made many mistakes while evolving on the earth, probably the worst has been to misidentify the origin of existence to be a monotheistic god who is good. Through the past twenty-five hundred years, this distorting error has been a cognitive deception for so many unfortunate individuals.

Like a delicious tasting but toxic fruit, the swallowed pleasant idea of a monotheistic god contains no real nourishment and is harmful, and should be regurgitated from where it originates, the human cerebral cortex of the brain. Portrayed as true, the artistic character of a monotheistic god is a false and toxic idea presented as a good fruit of human knowledge that continues to appeal to and be swallowed by many. Humans continue to swallow the seemingly good but actual noxious subjective knowledge of a monotheistic god. The knowledge is pleasant but is a detrimental delusion that for over two thousand years has continued to interest many people.

A great many individuals continue to obtain some minimal satisfaction from the subjective idea of a first father. A monotheistic god is a placebo, a sugar pill.

Once it is swallowed and digested, it bestows a subjective good feeling and healing affect. Worry and sadness are often reduced and psychosomatic conditions may be removed. Some identifiable good is obviously needed to veer conscious attention away from the real dualistic good and evil experiences of life. The notion of a guiding monotheistic god is for many people a good idea that persuades them in the direction of good and away from evil behaviors.

An increasing number of people find a first father god not to be a good fruit of human knowledge but find it to be a fruity idea that is most unappetizing and refuse to swallow it. Knowledge of a first father god is artistic and subjective, not realistic and objective. The idea of a monotheistic god while contributing some good to humans, has been and continues to be an overall self-inflicted curse that Middle East and western cultures have brought upon themselves. The artistic story of a monotheistic god is not comprehended to be word art and is mistaken for objective knowledge which yields a false fruit that poorly sustains and malnourishes humankind.

The other unfortunate knowledge obtained from the Garden of Eden story is the lack of it, the blatant monotheistic ignorance of a real animating and willing soul of life and its true origin as a continuation of the environment. A soul has not been made by any sort of human-like god. Inside the body is a partial conscious self and a predominantly subconscious soul that is a continuation of the energy particles immediately outside of the body in the environment. The soul as a dynamic continuation of energy particles is what bestows a resistance to destruction.

What the artistic fiction of the Garden of Eden story is really saying, is not that humans are separated from a good first father but are evolutionarily and biologically disadvantaged. Based on the findings of neuroscience, the cerebral cortex of the brain consists of fourteen billion neurons while the midbrain consists of seventy billion neurons. Human attention is often distracted by troubles, worries, struggles, and sufferings. This being so, humans have little knowledge of their own conscious self, and a spectrum from vague to no knowledge of the less conscious and subconscious soul.

The Garden of Eden story illustrates the dynamic contest between evolved dual systems. These are the secondary conscious cerebral cortex of the brain and the primary subconscious midbrain that functions for survival. The drift of the story is, it is difficult for the cerebral cortex to be good as the midbrain and body dynamic of the soul inclines to the excessive willing urges to survive known as evil. This is in part why the human artistic ability to imagine, places picture images of a first father in a space and time sequence, and thereby contrives a story of an authoritative monotheistic god.

Real Exodus

There are no artifacts to support the biblical story of the Exodus, the circa 1200 BCE mass fleeing of Moses and the Hebrew peoples into the Sinai Desert to escape the Egyptian ruler and his soldiers. The route of the supposed Exodus has been well excavated but to date not a single artifact has been recovered to substantiate the biblical tale. Like the Genesis story, the lack of artifact evidence suggests the Exodus is also an artistic metaphor of word art.

However, a real psychological exodus has occurred and can be discerned. Circa 500 BCE, biblical word artists ideated a monotheistic god as a pragmatic way to identify the origin of existence. The god is portrayed to dictate commandments as a way to direct the Hebrew group to good behaviors. What all humans share is not an external monotheistic god but a cerebral cortex of the brain that can imagine, make an image, ideate and can also subjectively accept a shared first father. It is true that humans have many shared forefathers but it is pure fiction there is a first father who is also a god that made all things to exist.

The Genesis word portrait story of a monotheistic god is an exodus, a way of fleeing that occurs only in the cerebral cortex of the brain when it imagines a first father for protection. A real exodus consists of a three-part dynamic of fleeing from:

- The external environment

-
- Other harmful life forms and aggressive humans
- A real and yet unrecognized midbrain and body dynamic of an internal animating soul.

Conscious attention occurring in the cerebral cortex and frontal lobe of the brain is frequently held captive by distracting external troubles in the environment, and by the internal troubling midbrain and body and its urging demands of a triune soul dynamic of hunger for food and water, sex and reproduction, and aggression. It is then that a real psychological exodus occurs when many flee to the refuge of a subjective ideated word portrait of a monotheistic god. The cerebral cortex finds a muddled way to subjective freedom from the real external environment and from the internal midbrain and body dynamic. It does this by imagining a first father god who can subjectively lead humans and free them from the troubles of existence. The existential problem of separation is that by accepting the origin of existence to be a first father, the environment and internal biological urging of a triune soul dynamic is completely ignored and to use a word from the Genesis story, is a curse.

The monotheistic maneuver of turning attention to a first father god has over time become a psychological fleeing and exodus from an individual captivity of troubles. Since the idea of a first father is so simple, it is today accepted by a majority of people on the earth. In fleeing to a monotheistic god who can resurrect a deceased body, the attention of an individual flees from and fails to recognize and comprehend a real animating and willing soul.

Monotheistic religions are a mass exodus, a fleeing from observation of a real internal dynamic of self and soul of life, and from a real supportive environment, to instead flee to the subjective idea and story of a first father. The fleeing by monotheistic individuals and groups occurs as an exodus from real experience to the subjective ideation and word portrait story of a first father god. The only real exodus is an internal fleeing of attention from the troubles present in the environment, the troubled conscious self, and the often troubling less conscious and subconscious soul.

For monotheistic religions, humans are soulless, they have only an animating spirit or breath and a free will that along with the physical body are mortal and can only be resurrected following death by an external first father god. The faith, belief, and tradition of monotheistic religions serve as a substitute for observation and investigation of real self and soul functions. An attentive meditative individual must practice observation of both the conscious self and subconscious soul. In turning attention to appeal to an external first father in an effort to survive, there is overlooking of what internally survives to exist in a dimensional afterlife. What remains after physical death, survives and flees as a willing soul in an exodus from the body and the earth to an afterlife dimension. Case study and anecdotal evidence suggest this occurs without any assistance from a monotheistic god.

The Hindu popular culture also made their own exodus of fleeing from the troubles of life and death into the artistic visual images concocted in the cerebral cortex of the brain and then sculpted and painted, and written about in word art stories about various gods and goddesses. In contrast, the exodus of the wise of India was to retreat to the forest ashram, away from the artistic images and spoken and written word portraits, to practice yoga and meditation as a way to observe and investigate brain and body functions. Through meditation they observed and reduced excess conscious attention to sensations, and stilled the distracting flow of picture images of now, past, and future. The practice of yoga postures aided meditation by reducing stress in the body. The wise forest dwellers found relief from life and death by finding the soul and they called it the *atma*, when experienced is said to be bliss. But the bliss that does arise is really freedom from the animating soul that animates life to survive as the willing urges of hunger for food, sex and reproduction, and aggression.

In contrast to Hindu religion, Siddhartha Gautama (circa 623-543 BCE) did not flee from troubles in the environment nor those located within the body by using his cerebral cortex to artistically imagine and ideate a first father god. He did not portray visually or write any word stories about any god or goddess.

Siddhartha Gautama did retreat to the forest where he practiced training attention to meditatively observe the brain and body dynamic of the conscious self and the subconscious soul. Following six years of effort, he reached his goal of nirvana, and in so doing became Buddha, the awakened one.

Soul Day

Who has the fortitude to relinquish the artistic word portrait of a monotheistic god, to honor and revere what is real and true? Certainly, only a brave few will be able to appreciate a first father to be a cultural subjective word art portrait of story. The ideation of a monotheistic god is an artistic effort to identify the origin of existence, and to feel cared for and protected. The subjective idea of a first father god is how some people find respite in the strife of life. A monotheistic day of worship is a way to briefly bask in the subjective idea of a first father god as a devised rest from earthly existence. The sabbath day of Saturday of Judaism, Sunday of Christianity, and Friday of Islam, provide a superficial rest from daily activities and turn attention to the origin of existence, a first father idolized to be a monotheistic god.

A holy day for the artistic word portrait of a first father god is a symptom of a failure for self and soul exploration and recognition of what really exists. Monotheistic religions do not recognize an animating soul, only a spirit or breath, a free will, and body. Each function is accepted to be nonspecial and mortal, and following death, must at some future time be restored to life by a first father during an anticipated special resurrection day.

The praise of a first father on a special day of the week is really a day of honoring the higher cerebral cortex functions of the human brain that can devise the word story origin of existence. Since the artistic word portrait of a monotheistic god is honored weekly on a special day, then it is only fair to honor a real animating soul that exists as a continuation of the earth. Soul Day should be a weekly time of recognizing that an animating soul exists and that it is a continuation of the environment.

The day should be celebrated by acknowledging a triune soul is real, supported by evidence based on inductive reasoning, observation, and study of its life support functions. Celebration of soul day must not be based on faith or tradition such as required for a monotheistic god.

Where humans come from is not a monotheistic god but a real animating soul that is a continuation of the earth. What is prominent and worshipped is subjective, an artistic word portrait of an intelligent and good monotheistic god. What is not recognized to exist is what is most true and objectively real, an animating less intelligent and subconscious soul that is both good and evil. A word art story of a monotheistic god elevates humans above what really animates them, an unnoticed triune soul that is a continuation of the environment that supports them. Many humans prefer their origin to be artistically portrayed with words and to be a first father god who is good and can help or punish the deserving.

Humans *en masse* will find it difficult to worship a real less conscious and subconscious soul as an urging force of hunger for food and water, sex and reproduction, and aggression. Humans prefer to worship a monotheistic god, subjectively imagined and existent only in the conscious intelligent cerebral cortex of the human brain and nowhere else. For monotheistic religions, no animating mechanism exists internally, only externally as an intelligent first father god. The less intelligent urges of a subconscious soul are not recognized to exist and the nonconscious and nonintelligent environment is not considered to be capable of animating life.

While ignored for an artistic story character of a monotheistic god, a real animating soul does exist within the human body. A soul is resistant to destruction and animates a physical body that eventually succumbs to accident, illness, aggression, ageing, and death. Behaviors of the soul are good for survival and worthy to be celebrated but are often harmful to the individual and easily disapproved of by the conscious self. Therefore, based on blind faith and tradition, it is an artistic word portrait of a first father god that is esteemed, revered, and worshipped.

Metaphorical monotheistic religions are soulless and conceal how life is a continuation of the environment. They actually have some support by empirical science that accepts life came from and is supported by the earth, yet it like monotheistic religion, also rejects the existence of an animating soul. A true disaster by both human endeavors to obtain reliable knowledge but instead distort a profound cosmological fact.

As a continuation of the energy particles of the environment, the soul is resistant to destruction and as anecdotal and case study evidence suggests, it may continue to exist after death. The soul is real and worthy of awe, reverence, and worship. Shrouded by the physical body, the covert animating function of the soul is for most very difficult to discern. Yet, its overt willing body behaviors are in plain sight for all to observe. Therefore, real and existent, there should be a weekly special day to honor the soul. The animating willing soul should be rightly honored and worshipped as a continuation of the willing-like energy particles of the earth and sun environment. Songs for the soul must be composed and sung on its special day of celebration and recognition to be a continuation from a real seething sea of energy particles of the environment.

At a minimum, Soul Day must be celebrated at least once yearly. Perhaps the single most appropriate day during the year is near or on Earth Day which occurs annually on April 22. The earth, not a monotheistic god, is the nearest supportive relative and origin of life. A first father is a subjective work of word art and deserves to be discarded, while the soul is real and deserves to be regarded and celebrated.

The days of Friday, Saturday, and Sunday are celebrated weekly by monotheistic religions by turning attention to a monotheistic god and conducting rituals. Probably the most appropriate weekday available to celebrate the animating soul is Monday, originally meaning "moon day." Monday should be set aside to weekly recognize the animating soul in humans, and to revere and celebrate it to be a real continuation of a sea of energy particles of the earth and sun environment, and as such is resistant to destruction.

A special weekly day of celebrating the soul should include moderating its triune functions of hunger for food and water, sex and reproduction, and aggression. The cerebral cortex is located higher above the lower midbrain and body. Therefore, Soul Day should also be a weekly time of recognizing not an ideated first father god but the ability of the evolved cerebral cortex of the brain, the conscious self, to moderate and balance the less conscious and subconscious midbrain and body dynamic of animating and willing functions of the triune soul.

European Soul

Catholic Christianity and the Church of England celebrate All Saints day on November 1, and what is popularly called Commemoration of All the Faithful Departed on November 2. It is not a day of celebrating all the departed, only those faithful who temporarily reside in Purgatory and not in Hell. Protestant religions widened the day to remember all those who have died, and hence gave it the name of All Souls Day.

The English derived prayer published in The New England Primer circa 1784 and taught through the years by parents to children, does not mention a spirit (Latin spiritus, breath) but a soul as the surviving essence of an individual.

"Now I lay me down to sleep,
I pray thee, Lord, my soul to keep;
If I should die before I wake,
I pray thee, Lord, my soul to take."

The Old and New Testaments do not mention a word for soul. The word soul is European, from English *sawol*, and German *sela*, Norse *sala*, Old Saxon *seola*. The Nordic word refers to a process of what animates life and returns to its origin. The word for soul seems to have meant, "coming from and going to water," meaning that for Nordic peoples, souls came from the surface dimension or depth of lakes or ponds, and returned them.

The soul may have been associated with spring-fed waters. The soul could also have been related to the animating waves or flowing surface of a pond or lake, and perhaps associated with ethereal fog that animates and forms mysteriously on the surface of water and soon dissipates. It was probably suspected that the rarified and wraith-like animated fog came from, appeared and disappeared by returning to the water. The Nordics observed fog rising from a water surface to suspend in air, damp to touch, the dew and rain falls on plants that absorb it through leaves and roots, the essence of its moistness needed like food to live.

The reflection of a person on the still surface of water is certainly unique, and the ability to reflect images is special and found nowhere else in the environment. Seeing the reflective image of a person in the water, simple analogical reasoning may have been that life came from the water, and also held the image of life in its watery surface or depth following death. The clear reflecting surface may have served as an analogical representation of a dimensional opening and entrance to another continuing and ethereal existence, an idea supported by glimpsing fluid-like images of the departed during dreams and visions.

Simple reasoning may have generated the idea that the soul or image reflection of the dead person returned to the water and continued to exist therein following death. The image contained in water really points to what it really consists of that saves the soul, a seething sea of energy particles of which it is a continuation and therefore resistant to destruction.

Water is essential for life and it has been observed that plants, animals, and humans perish much more quickly without water than when deprived of food. Water seeps into soil from rain and collects in rivers and streams, and in lakes, ponds, and bogs. Water is a continuation of and is supported by the earth that consists of recurring cycles of day and night, weather, and seasonal behaviors. These cyclic behaviors probably contributed inspiration for the reincarnation myths of the Celts and Greeks.

Edward Conklin

The Indo-European analogical tradition of an animating soul is real and true while the breath or spirit of a monotheistic first father that animates mortal life is false and an artistic word portrait representation. That humans have an animating spirit or breath from a first father god is the Middle East story tradition. The view of humans having an animating soul as a continuation of water and the earth that contains it is the indigenous Indo-European tradition. In the Nordic *sala* and *seola* tradition, the soul came from water that is supported by a nonvisible but sensed sea of energy particles that constitute the earth and is the real origin of life.

Perhaps the soul tradition associated with water may serve as partial explanation for the presence of human bodies found in lake, pond, and bog areas. The practice dates from circa 8000 BCE to 1400 CE, and what are known as "bog bodies are found in the Nordic countries of Denmark, Germany, Netherlands, England, Scotland, and Ireland. Speculating, it may have been that the body along with its animating soul was returned to a clear watery dimension that analogically represented an ethereal afterlife. The Nordics have been nearly correct through the centuries and continue to be so; a soul saves to another dimension while the artistic word portrait of the first father god and resurrection advocated by monotheistic religions, only subjectively saves.

In the biblical Genesis story, a monotheistic god breathed on the surface of the waters of existence as a way to account for its animation of waves and flowing movement. (Genesis 1:2) The mythic story of the first father's spirit or breath blowing over the waters to animate them is just so much clumsy superstition, as is the breath or spirit breathed into humans (Genesis 2:7) to animate them and yet is mortal and dies along with the body.

The Genesis first father used his mouth to talk the environment into existence, to blow and move the waves of water in the Red Sea, and to blow life into the first human. The described blowing by a first father god is really blowhard authors giving precedence to males by emphasizing the first human of existence to be male.

That a first father god blew on the water to move it, talked the environment and life into existence, and blew plain air and a free will into the first human body, is a blowhard story that artistically boasts and brags about a male beginning of existence.

Praise

The word portrait of a monotheistic god is a way of representing and praising the artistic ability of the human cerebral cortex of the brain. It is comforting for many people to sit or stand with others in a monotheistic worship service of a synagogue, church, or mosque to honor the word portrait of a first father god made by the cerebral cortex of the brain as an artistic way of identifying the origin of existence.

The praise given to a first father really belongs to the cerebral cortex of the brain that artistically imagines the god to exist in a word portrait of story. Better and more real is it to sit or stand on the soil and be amazed by a real animating soul within the body that is a continuation of the energy particles of the earth and sun. The real origin of life is an animating soul that is a continuation of the energy particles of the environment. The original sin of biblical separation, is to give credit for the origin of life to a monotheistic first father god story, rather than to an internal animating soul that is a continuation of a real environment.

The earth rotating and suspended in infinite space is a real human home. Difficult to discern that extending beyond the earth may also exist some sort of near-earth dimension and afterlife. Evidence suggests that souls continue to exist rooted in the energy of a near-earth dimension, and as some anecdotal and case studies suggest, may continue to exist and communicate with those still rooted physically in an earthly dimension. The evidence for soul survival is slight as suggested by double blind studies of mediums, anecdotal and case study reports of near-death experiences, childhood reincarnation memories, comforting after death visits by deceased relatives and friends, and many sightings and sensing of ghosts.

Supported by observational and experiential evidence, death is the completing of a circuit, leaving an earthly home and transiting to an ethereal home. From an afterlife dimension, the soul resistant to destruction, may one day return to earth, an act suggested by anecdotal and case study evidence, and that may reflect not only earthly evolution but also a greater scope of continuing evolution. Humans are born with innate genetic biological traits of inheritance. Some may be born with previous acquired subconscious picture images and willing habit patterns, in other words, are reborn or reincarnated.

A soul is rewarded by obtaining what it wants, mainly food and water, sex and reproduction, and aggression. A soul is punished by what it is, a habit pattern of restless dynamic willing that as a continuation of energy particles of the environment is therefore resistant to destruction. A soul may continue to exist repeatedly until the conscious self recognizes its less conscious and subconscious soul patterns of picture images and willing, and tires of and makes the effort to reduce and resolve them. Individual life consists of patterns of waking and sleeping, active and resting, awake and sleeping, and these lesser patterns are repeated in the greater cyclic pattern of life and death.

Soulless

Monotheistic religions are soulless and tout only a spirit or breath and a free will and these are both treated as mortal along with the body and must be resurrected by a first father god. The human determination to continue in existence is bolstered by imagining there is a willing first father god that helps humans to survive life and death. A monotheistic god is a way to insulate humans from the environment and to provide comfort from unexpected and harmful experiences.

In monotheistic religions, the body is deprecated as it is easily observed that it is fragile, gets diseases, is easily injured, ages, and dies. The inner dynamic of the body is plagued with psychological disorders, an impaired intelligence quotient, lack of sufficient education, and is fearful of many situations.

In the Middle East it was adjudged and generally accepted that nothing exists within the body that is worthwhile and that can survive death. What is valuable can only exist outside of the body and not inside of it. Therefore, whoever wants to continue to exist, must direct their attention to a monotheistic god who can resurrect the body to live again.

Despite the naïve attitude of monotheistic religions, an animating soul does exist within the human body. A soul is super natural, it transcends the body as it is a continuation of unseen energy particles of the surround environment. Coming from a singular nonlocal cosmological force, energy particles form the local environment and its willing-like change, of which life is a continuation. Human willing is a conscious, less conscious, and subconscious direct continuation of energy particles of the willing-like change of the environment. The environment and life have come from a dimension not inhabited by a monotheistic god but by metaphysical energy, a dimension of reality totally unknown during the time of the founding of monotheistic religions. Time for a paradigm shift away from artistic story to what is real and detectable.

Soulless Versus Soul

The two largest religious orientations of the earthly population are, worship of a monotheistic god and acceptance of reincarnation. Based on recent statistics, the population of the earth is estimated and categorized into the following percentages:

Orientation	**%**
Monotheism	55
Reincarnation	22
Folk Religions	6
Not Affiliated	16
(Pew Research Center)	

Folk Religions consist of tribal or small local religious traditions. The category of Not Affiliated are atheists, sceptics, and humanists.

Perhaps add one percent individual beliefs to complete the total of one-hundred percent. Yet, how dismal are these figures? Sad but true, over half of the population of the earth accepts the subjective word portrait of a monotheistic first father god to be objective and real.

Monotheistic religions are soulless religions. Humans have an animating breath (Latin spiritus, breath) and a free will, yet these are mortal as is the body and must be resurrected by a first father god. Those who promote and those who accept a monotheistic god are really referring to the cerebral cortex of the brain where the subjective artistic idea is imagined. A monotheistic god represents praise of the higher cerebral cortex of the brain that subjectively ideates the god to exist objectively, while the simultaneous role of first father represents the sexual reproduction of many forefathers.

Nearly twenty-five percent of the human population accept reincarnation and recognize the soul and its resistance to destruction, though variations exist of what it may consist. There also exist many experiential anecdotal comments and case studies of both average and notable people who accept the dynamic of past lives and reincarnation.

Soul Musing

The cerebral cortex of the average human brain does not like to think of where it comes from as less knowing and less conscious and does not like to dwell on the notion that the animating origin of life also exists in a perishable body. What the cerebral cortex of the monotheistic brain prefers, is to ideate a special greater intelligence that made the environment and that externally animates the living body.

Vaguely sensed by many humans, is that despite the struggle and many evils of existence, there is an energy that constitutes life and it is relative to and is a continuation of the environment. The First Law of Thermodynamics states that energy is neither created nor destroyed.

This confirmed fact of energy by the science of physics is what is represented by monotheistic religions as a monotheistic god who is said to be eternal.

Material forms are long lasting as they consist internally of energy particles. The human body though not long lasting, also consists of elements of energy that animate it, and its continuance of willing known as a soul is long lasting. Individual willing is resistant to destruction and needs not to be strengthened by pairing it with the subjective ideation of a monotheistic god. A human willing soul does not need to be saved, it truly must be reduced, moderated, and resolved. Individuals must save themselves from the soul.

There is a real willing that continues on seemingly forever but it is not the will of a monotheistic god. A first father god is an artistic word portrait of story and exists only subjectively. Rather, it is the human willing soul that is resistant to destruction and can and does continue on, not in a linear direction but in circles and cycles until resolved. Some people who are known as New Age advocates, maintain that reincarnation does occur and that humans do return to perfect what they regard to be a good soul to even further goodness. This is a mistaken idea.

Those who seek a good human soul are far from comprehension of a soul as it functions only for the good of survival. The perfection of the soul is relative, not to save it but to reduce and to be rid of it, and only individual knowledge can accomplish the task. The soul is a predominantly less conscious and subconscious function of midbrain and body, and only the conscious cerebral cortex of the brain can exert the effort required to comprehend and untangle the mess that is life and death. Rather than imagine a monotheistic god who can subjectively help humans, it is the existential task of each individual now and forever to observe and comprehend the human self and triune soul.

Trouble

Based on the best estimate of neuroscience, the human conscious cerebral cortex (self) consists of approximately fourteen percent of total brain neurons, and the less conscious and subconscious midbrain (soul) function is eighty-six percent of brain neurons. The conscious self, functions to make picture images of now, past, and future from sensations. The subconscious soul functions as an often-troubling triune dynamic of biological urges as hunger for food and water, sex and reproduction, and aggression. The self is a conscious function and the urges of the soul are less conscious and subconscious. The dynamic of the soul exists as a triune whole and also distinct; each is a gradation of the other and yet function differently and separately. The three exist as distinct realities, conscious and subconscious, and connecting them is less conscious whose function may be to remember or to forget. The subconscious soul intrudes upon, influences, and demands the conscious cerebral cortex to furnish picture images and to will for what it wants to acquire.

The conscious self is often troubled by the less conscious and subconscious soul with its triune demands of hunger for food and water, sex and reproduction, and aggression. The environment is troublesome and relationships with other humans are often troubled. To the many troubling experiences of life, the conscious cerebral cortex of the monotheistic brain responds by ideating a first father god to reduce or remove the troubles of existence. Yet, this psychological maneuver is only subjectively effective. Evidence suggests that even death may not remove the troubles of life. Anecdotal and case study reports suggest that the troubles of life may continue to exist for an individual after physical death. The ample evidence consists of near-death experiences, childhood reincarnation memories, anecdotal accounts of after death visits by deceased relatives and friends, and many sightings and sensing of ghosts.

Shunning

The practice of shunning is defined as:

"To refuse to accept socially, to avoid having contact with, to stay away from and not to interact with or acknowledge someone."

The Garden of Eden is a myth, a metaphorical story of shunning, whereby the cerebral cortex of the brain shuns the midbrain and body functions. The story represents an expulsion of midbrain and body functions and they are forbidden to enter the sanctified area of the cerebral cortex of the brain, especially when it is occupied by the ideational word art portrait of a first father god.

In the biblical Genesis story, the first humans are metaphorically portrayed as obtaining a fruit of good and evil knowledge from a tree made by the first father god. The good knowledge represents that obtained from the cerebral cortex and conscious self. The evil knowledge represents that which is obtained from the less conscious and subconscious midbrain and body, the innate dynamic which is a triune soul as a hunger for food and water, sex and reproduction, and aggression. The duality of knowledge contained in a single tree and its fruit, represents the innate bifurcation of knowledge into cerebral cortex and midbrain and body, conscious and subconscious, and self and soul.

The intelligent god alias cerebral cortex, banished and shunned the first humans, alias the midbrain and body dynamic of a real animating soul as urging forces of hunger for food, sex and reproduction, and aggression. To be exiled and shunned by a first father really means the cerebral cortex of the brain expels and refuses to allow the midbrain and body functions to take precedence over its own. The subjective artistic imagery of story knowledge of a monotheistic god replaces any chance of objective knowledge of a real animating and willing soul. The cerebral cortex of the monotheistic brain, alias the first father god of story, refuses to even recognize the troublesome midbrain and body dynamic of an animating soul. By ideating and writing about a monotheistic god, the cerebral cortex ignores an animating soul and retains all ability for animating life to its own functions. It is the character of a monotheistic god that must be banished by recognizing it to be subjective word art. The banished animating willing soul must be recognized and accepted back into the garden ground, there to take its rightful and real place as the true animator and progenitor of life and death.

Garden Growth

Artist scribes of the Genesis story ideated a story about a first father god who made the environment and a garden for humans to care for and protect. Compatible with their daily assigned task of gardening, the first humans like many have since done, developed an interest in cultivating their inner growth of knowledge.

The first humans, having a basic knowledge of plant care, managed the task of cultivating the Garden of Eden. Eventually, maybe from boredom, the first humans turned their attention to acquiring more knowledge to utilize in caring for their own internal growth. Instead of posing questions and getting answers from the monotheistic god, the first humans instead chose to ingest a fruit containing some of the god's good knowledge but it also contained some of his evil knowledge.

Unknown to the first humans, there were two fertile gardens to care for, the one external and the other internal. The growth of the human self and comprehension of the soul can be likened to a garden, and this is why to this day, inner growth expressed as outer behaviors, are cultivated and guided by manners, customs, tradition, morals, ethics, laws, and education. Like managing the growth of beneficial garden plants, internal growth of good within humans must be nourished, pruned, and protected, and any evil or nonbeneficial growth must be removed.

The seeds of nonbeneficial evil weeds are difficult to see but when they sprout into seedling plants and begin to grow and are observed and identified, they can then more easily be pulled and removed from the internal garden of self and soul. The internal garden is where sensations grow into picture images of now, past, and future, and where conscious willing grows into behaviors, and where subconscious urging grows into hunger for food and water, sex and reproduction, and aggression. Everyone must perform the existential task of cultivating internal good growth and removing the nonbeneficial and excessive evils of weed growth.

But like many who have a "black thumb," meaning their effort at cultivating and growing of plants results in them withering and dying, so too many people lack skill and are inept at cultivating internal growth of self and soul. However, the evidence of case study reports of near-death experiences, childhood reincarnation memories, anecdotal accounts of after death visits by deceased relatives and friends, and many sightings and sensing of ghosts, suggest that caring for internal individual growth is a long-lasting task of humans that may continue through life and after physical death.

Cultivate Your Garden

A lack of clarity and knowledge may be deemed to be a real evil of ignorance. When biblical writers creatively ideated a good first father, this artistic act simultaneously created a lack of clear knowledge and an onset of ignorance by confusing subjective ideation with objective reliable knowledge. Simultaneously, when the idea of a first father god first happened to a word artist scribe who wrote the Genesis story of a first father god, there also occurred an onset of ignorance in discerning the inner dynamic of the human self and soul.

Like prolific plants, sensations, picture images, willing, and urging forces of hunger for food and water, sex and reproduction, and aggression, crowd the limited conscious attention span of the cerebral cortex of the brain. When attention to sensations is reduced, picture images of now, past, and future are reduced, and when willing is lessened and moderated, the paradisiacal garden ground of the human dynamic of self and soul is revealed to a persistent seeker in its primal and pristine clarity.

The French writer-philosopher Francois Marie Arouet, better known by his *nom de plume* of Voltaire (1694-1778) was outspoken and critical of the practices and teachings of monotheistic religions of Judaism, Christianity, and Islam. Voltaire seems to have accepted the view of an unknown god to explain the origin of existence but it had nothing to do with the tradition of monotheistic religions which he harshly criticized on occasions.

Voltaire gave philosophical advice to his fellow humans when in his work *Candide*, (1759) he wrote the words, *Il faut cultiver son jardin*, which translates to English as, "cultivate your garden." Humans are innately interested in cultivating beneficial growth of plants and trees in the environment, and are also just as interested in the growth of financial security, family, and the inner growth of knowledge of brain and body.

Good beneficial plants are cultivated yet nonbeneficial weed seeds arrive by chance, sprout, grow, and if not attended to, soon crowd out useful growth. Humans are innate gardeners and have the existential task of cultivating beneficial growth both externally and internally. The cerebral cortex of the brain must cultivate internal good plants and remove the behavioral weeds of evil growth. Unfortunately for humankind, each individual must be responsible and do this on their own, rather than subjectively ideate and rely on a monotheistic first father god.

Middle East cultures developed to value cultivation of what was outside of them, the growth of food plants and caring for the growth of livestock and building of structures. They lacked a method of observing and cultivating what is inside. There was a failure to develop an internal method of introspection, of meditative observation and cultivating the good, and of not letting grow by weeding away what is bad and evil. Instead, their attention was subjectively directed outward by monotheistic artist scribes to the word portrait of a first father god. *Un mauvais sort.*

Life Lesson

The life lesson presented in the biblical Garden of Eden story, is that humans on the spectrum of willing and knowledge, must cultivate what is higher and shun what is lower. The cerebral cortex of the brain is located above the lower midbrain and body of humans, the dynamic of which is a triune soul. The general meaning of the story is to cultivate cerebral cortex knowledge, and to banish or reduce midbrain and body knowing urges.

The cerebral cortex with its ability for conscious attention to sensations, and the making of picture images of now, past, and future, is often unaccepting of the midbrain and body knowledge of urges for eating, digesting and expelling of food and urine, sex and reproduction, and aggression. The dynamic of the triune urges is an innate ability to survive life and death. The story metaphor poignantly means that the cerebral cortex of the brain, the conscious self, must focus attention on and learn more about its own functions and the subconscious midbrain and body dynamic of an animating and willing triune soul.

Those who worship a monotheistic god really worship the subjective idea generated and rooted in the cerebral cortex of the brain. When monotheistic oriented humans identify where life comes from to be a first father, they simultaneously ignore an internal animating soul, the external environment, and of course lacking ability to perceive atoms and electrons, fail to notice a sea of quantum energy particles of the earth and sun. Not a willing first father but the willing soul is a real progenitor of life that is a continuation of the environment.

Rather than fixating on the word art of a monotheistic god, there must be cultivated a focus of attention on a real triune soul that is a continuation of a shared environment. In this way, lower less conscious and subconscious soul knowledge of urges can be accepted, integrated, and welcomed back into the primal garden ground and union with the cerebral cortex, alias, the banishing monotheistic first father god. Conscious attention can reduce the shunning of the midbrain and body by the cerebral cortex.

Tension of differing functions will always exist between the cerebral cortex and the midbrain and body, yet this is as it has evolved to be. The cerebral cortex, alias the conscious self, is a latecomer, indeed is a prodigy of the more ancient midbrain and body function and dynamic of an animating willing soul. The soul is in turn a prodigy and continuation of a seething sea of energy particles of the environment and a cosmological force that moves the universe and ever exists on its own.

The Garden of Eden represents the primal ground that existed prior to the story imagery of a monotheistic god. It is the nonlocal ground of all grounds from which all goes forth including countless galaxies, stars, planets, sun and earth. From a sea of energy particles of the local environment, grow microscopic viruses and bacteria, plant, and animal life, and the cerebral cortex of the human brain from which grows the artistic story images of a first father god to poorly explain it all.

Soulish

It probably makes more sense to say that the human condition is soulish as what is wanted is more for the soul, such as food and water, sex and reproduction, and aggression. This makes more sense than to say a person is selfish as the self is most reasonable of the two functions and more than not answers to and obeys the triune soul. Always in the background lurking, the soul is ready to locate and consume food and water, to have sex and to reproduce, and to express aggression. Not a monotheistic god but the subconscious triune soul ever governs the conscious self, and rules life and death.

Monotheistic religions reinforce willing of the conscious self by creatively ideating and writing a word portrait story of a first father god. Human life consists predominantly of lower soulish behaviors of the midbrain and body and less of higher god-like ideating behaviors of the cerebral cortex of the brain, alias the conscious self.

Soul Litter

Does a human soul exist? If so, of what does it consist? Where does it come from, and does it survive death? The God & Soul Theory asserts that a human soul does exist and that it is possible to observe and comprehend it. The dynamic function of the soul contributes to the survival of life, and it is, to borrow a word triune, meaning singular yet has three dynamic interdependent functions. The soul dynamic is a trinity of less conscious and subconscious willing urges for food, sex and reproduction, and aggression that enable life to survive.

Sensations do not long endure, picture images do not long endure, conscious willing does not long endure but subconscious willing of the human midbrain and body long endures as habit patterns. Willing habits tend to endure and repeat as a pattern in the body and as a continuation of a sea of energy particles of the cyclical environment, may continue to endure out of the body. Anecdotal and case study evidence suggests, willing habits may continue to endure out of the body in a substrate field of energy particles. The body dies but habitual willing may externalize from the body at the time of death to continue, and perhaps to inhabit or indwell another body. While the biological body is limited by changing time, what animates it is a soul that is long-lasting and resistant to destruction.

The basis for experiences of love and hate reflect the soul, the urging of sex and reproduction and aggression, rounding out with hunger for food and water to be a triune function. Willing is impressed, suffused, and permeated with residue remnants of sensate images. Picture images are dependent on and adhesive to willing that in excess do litter the less conscious and subconscious soul with patterns not easily able to be un-patterned.

The triune soul is a continuation of the seething energy particles of the earth and sun environment and is therefore resistant to destruction. Through experience, the soul is imbued with subconscious habit patterns of behavior and picture images, and these are resistant to destruction. As a subconscious survival function of hunger for food and water, sex and reproduction, and aggression, the soul often resists efforts of direction, modification, and reduction made by the conscious self.

Supported by and as a continuation of the energy particles of the environment, the soul animates life and enables it to survive. To survive life experiences, the animating subconscious soul accumulates a dynamic of habit patterns of efforts and images. The animating and sustaining efforts of the soul do not cease at the time of death but continue to exist. The soul consists of behavioral habits and the habit of producing picture images to guide willing behaviors.

Ladened with a majority of habit patterns of behaviors and a minority of picture images, cause the subconscious soul to repeat and have a circular trajectory. The ability of the soul to repeat is a continuation of the repetitions of the environment including, weather patterns, seasons, and planet rotation of day and night and revolution around the sun, and the unobserved circular orbit of energy particles.

During a short or long lifespan, the subconscious soul in willing for food and water, sex and reproduction, and aggression develops habitual behaviors, and habits of preferred picture images that adhere to its urging efforts for survival. Therefore, subconscious behavioral habits and at least some remnant conscious picture images of preferred people, places, and things survive.

The soul has an adhesive quality to its main cosmological function of surviving. The soul dynamic, a continuation of energy, is resistant to destruction and as such it retains and contains a less conscious and subconscious maze of willing behavioral habits. Included is the repetitive habit of the conscious self to make picture images of external objects in internal space and time. Life is a wandering through a dynamic maze of self and soul.

Analogically, when a rock is crushed by pounding, it is reduced to random loose observable particles of sand and dust, and unobservable but proven to exist atom and electron particles. The particles are soon blown away and scattered by the wind and washed away by rain and water. Unlike the stone, the human body consists of conscious willing efforts and habit patterns of picture images, and less conscious and subconscious willing behavior patterns for food and water, sex, and aggression.

As a continuation of energy particles, the soul resists destruction and coheres, stays glued together as habit patterns. The animating and willing essence is conserved and wants to continue to survive and even to live again. A soul while performing the vital animating function of surviving is also, while not thought of as such, subject to excess clutter or litter.

But what can possibly clutter or litter a metaphysical human soul? Many are not aware of the soul's existence and of the individual responsibility and existential need to initiate some cleansing of such a metaphysical function. Both anecdotal and case study evidence suggest that the human willing soul resists destruction and is capable of restarting and continuing in another body. Those who may experience a glimmer of reincarnation memories, sit to train attention to focus and to meditate and to reduce distractions so as to better observe and clean up the litter of habit behaviors and picture images and thereby reduce the potential dynamic for a reincarnating soul.

Prior to efforts to cleanse the soul, the conscious self must be cleansed of excess distractions of sensations by training attention. Behavioral habits and picture images limit an individual to what is known and generally nonthreatening and safe. This is the soul's subconscious urge to survive by retaining picture images of certain experiences to have or avoid. There must be a meditative reducing of picture images of now, past, and future, and of changeable conscious willing. Accomplishing this, the triune soul of excessive clutter and litter of images and biological urges of hunger for food, sex, and aggression can then be moderated and cleansed.

The cerebral cortex consists of sixteen billion neurons that comprise fourteen percent of the brain. Midbrain functions comprise seventy billion and eighty-six percent of the total eighty-six billion neurons. Following this ratio, the conscious self and the subconscious soul probably retains near the same proportion. While difficult to cleanse the self, it is much more difficult and even dangerous to cleanse the less conscious and subconscious soul as it is much stronger and can distort the functions of the conscious self. Each individual proceeds at their own risk and very few succeed.

The soul resistant to destruction, does not take kindly to a reducing of its function to survive. During the cleansing of the self and soul, there can be observed and comprehended that there might also be undertaken, a gradual ascetic discipline to deconstruct or un-save both the conscious self and the subconscious dynamic of the triune soul.

This will require discipline and a long-term commitment for any interested individual.

Cleanup

An individual certainly cannot appeal to a monotheistic god to assist in cleansing a person's soul. The monotheistic god did not endow humans with a soul but only with a breath (Latin spiritus, breath) and a free will, both of which like the body are mortal. The only real way to cleanse the soul is to meditatively see and comprehend that its primary essence consists of dynamic urges and willing efforts for food and water, sex and reproduction, and aggression that must be moderated and reduced.

The main attribute of the triune soul is its resistance to destruction, and through experience it is imbued with habitual behavior patterns of willing and the habit of making internal picture images of external objects in a space and time sequence. Behavioral habits and familiar picture images are comforting and conscious attention can find refuge from unfamiliar, sudden, or threatening experiences.

It is difficult to rely on individual efforts to cleanse the cluttered and littered hallowed ground of the soul that is resistant to destruction as it is a continuation of a seething sea of energy particles of the cosmos. The monotheistic majority take the easy way out and accept on faith, belief, and tradition that a first father god will help save them from the cluttering and littering sins of individual life. Yet it is quite certain that a monotheistic god is a subjective work of word art, and when mistaken to be objective, is a delusion that cannot unclutter and remove litter from the lives of individuals.

The first father god of monotheistic religions is a faulty subjective way to prevent or remove clutter and litter of the individual mortal physical brain and body having a spirit or breath and a free will. In monotheistic religions, individual clutter and litter are ambivalent violations of dictated commandments, the ethical and moral sins of separation from a good god.

The use of a first father god functions as a superficial larger conscience that keeps a subjective eye on a monotheistic believing individual only from the inside of the cerebral cortex of the brain. For monotheistic religions, the brain and body will not be resurrected if the omniscient first father god knows of any clutter and litter of evil behaviors committed by the individual. A greater monotheistic god is a subjective and quasi-therapeutic artistic use of a word portrait to prevent ethical and moral violations and is a poor prohibitive effort to prevent ambivalent clutter and litter of the brain and body.

In contrast to monotheistic religious teachings, Sigmund Freud (1856-1939) Jewish atheist and medical doctor, developed the therapeutic method of psychoanalysis to explore the conscious ego, superego of conscience, and the dynamic unconscious Id by utilizing the technique of free association and dream analysis. In his work, Freud sought to correct the monotheistic delusion of a father fixation, a subjective and neurotic way to identify the origin of existence and to obtain care and protection. Though Freud did not accept the view of a soul within humans, psychoanalysis is a way of removing the litter of subconscious habits and clutter of traumatic picture images located in the unconscious Id.

Fritz Perls (1893-1970) Jewish born, atheist, psychiatrist and psychotherapist, developed the therapeutic technique of Gestalt Therapy which he wrote about in several books. One of his works published in 1969 just prior to his death, is entitled, *In and Out the Garbage Pail*. An apropos title as it discusses Gestalt Therapy dynamics of pulling out stored habit memories and through confrontation and role playing to resolve and discard the ineffective and distorting behaviors to the garbage bin.

Both Psychoanalysis and Gestalt Therapy are therapeutic ways of cleaning up the litter of an unrecognized and unmentioned soul of subconscious habits and picture images. In a sense, as modern Jewish sons, Freud and Perls both atone for their forebear's guilt in the development, acceptance, and use of the untherapeutic externalized monotheistic god.

Both have surpassed the primitive past dynamic of their shared cultural heritage by their courage in exploring the unknown terrain of the dynamic human psyche and behaviors.

Undo

Humans get overly comfortable with life, forgetting that it is only one half of existence and that the other half is death. The soul knows and its triune knowledge is how to survive, expressed as urges of hunger for food and water, sex and reproduction, and aggression. Death is a transition not to a monotheistic god but to a dimension of energy; not a first father but only energy saves. Suggested by anecdotal and case study evidence, energy patterns survive death and can reconnect to a biological cycle to continue evolutionary development. The soul survives by what it is, a continuation of a seething sea of energy particles of the environment and the formation of subconscious habit patterns.

Empirical science says there is no observational or testable evidence for the claim that habit patterns of behavior can exist without a physical body. Not to be so easily dismissed are countless anecdotal accounts and case study evidence. At least some reasonable doubt exists and lingers as to whether anecdotal evidence of individual experience should be completely discarded as imagination or intentional fraud.

A way to undo the habit patterns of the soul is meditation, a focus of attention that can remove the ties that bind. Meditation practice moderates both conscious and subconscious willing for sensations and for picture images of food, sex and reproduction, and aggression. Faith and belief in an external animator that will undo all human problems large and small, is much easier than individual efforts and time required to moderate and resolve internal animating urges of a triune soul. Yet, to rely on a monotheistic god to undo difficulties and make life better is a colossal mistaken idea.

Meditation and Dissociation

The conscious self begins the process of meditation by training attention to focus on a particular internal sensation of now, such as breathing. By so doing there occurs a temporary mild dissociation from external sensations of seeing, hearing, smelling, tasting, and touching.

Reducing attention to picture images of now, past, and future, there occurs a further mild dissociation from the content of the conscious self. Abiding in this mild poised stage of dissociation from the conscious functions of the self, less conscious and subconscious discomforts of the body are noticed along with the difficult to dissociate from internal urges of hunger for food and thirst for water, sex and reproduction, and aggression. The individual meditator must reduce willing for food, sex, and aggression but not to excess, so as to maintain the mild disassociation of poise.

Urges and Images

Relief from life can be obtained by a subjective belief in the objective existence of a monotheistic god. The only real and certain relief from life is the dimension of death where the picture images and urges acquired through experience of living may remain intact as a habit pattern of subconscious willing efforts to survive. A focus of attention during meditation is needed to observe this phenomenal reality. Prior to death, the task of life is to moderate the conscious self and the subconscious soul patterns that are resistant to destruction and may remain as images and urges for times and places. Residual picture images of the conscious self, derive their resistance to destruction from their affinity with and dependence on, the subconscious triune soul.

The triune urges of the soul absorb images to a relative surface depth but do not imbue it completely, only superficially. Meditation reduces the urges of the soul from binding with the self and its picture images of objects in space and time. Less conscious and subconscious willing for sensations of food, sex, and aggression, places objects in a space and time sequence of conscious picture images.

These forceful urges are a continuation of a sea of energy particles, in turn a continuation of a cosmological force that moves the universe. Practicing meditation reduces attention to conscious sensations and picture images of the self, and to less conscious and subconscious urges of the soul, and results in a clarity that can observe and comprehend both.

The nexus where urges and images meet, is arrived at with steady attention to prolong the distinct vision of the two, of the self as distinct from and dependent on the soul. The images of the conscious self, and urgings of the soul, are held in abeyance, neither is dominant over the other. The self is not out of control with rampant images of objects in space and time, and the soul urges are not out of control for food, sex, and aggression. From the abeyance of images and urges, and through consistent effort over time to reduce habit patterns, comes clarity and a touching of equilibrium and a relative existential peace of freedom.

Misplace

Much of life is spent in getting what is wanted, in keeping what is wanted, and the remainder of time is spent in getting rid of what is not wanted. Fortunately, most things are located where they should be in life and work relatively well most of the time. Yet, a lot of things are misplaced, they are either where they should not be or are not where they should be. Much of the effort of life is to get something to a place where it belongs, or to remove it from a place where it does not belong. A lot of time and effort are spent in life to get something to where it should be, or to remove something from a place where it should not be. From this twin dynamic come satisfactions and also the frustrations, temper tantrums, and aggressions of life.

Monotheistic religions misplace the origin of existence. They fit human origin into a place where it does not belong, the story character of a first father rather than a sea of energy particles of the environment. Monotheistic authorities attempt to convince those who will listen, to place their attention, faith, and trust in a first father god. Human trust is betrayed when it is placed in a monotheistic god.

A first father is not realistic but is a subjective and artistic word portrait story of the origin of existence. Attention to a monotheistic god is misplaced and must instead be focused on where life does originate, the visible environment composed of a seething sea of nonvisible but sensed energy particles.

Monotheistic faith and trust are also misplaced in a future resurrection of the breath, free will, and body by a first father god. Faith and trust must instead be placed in an animating soul within the human body. The soul is a triune urging and willing of hunger for food and water, sex and reproduction, and aggression, and as a continuation of energy particles of the environment, it is resistant to destruction.

Trick

The word trick is defined as:

"A simple feat of magic or optical illusion intended to amuse. An act or words intended to achieve a result in a deceptive or fraudulent way. To cheat or deceive, to play a practical joke on someone. An attempt to get someone to do something foolish or to act carelessly."

Monotheism is a trick, a misdirection of attention to the spoken or written word portrait of a first father god. A metaphorical god is subjective word art portrayed as objective, and is therefore intended to deceive and is a fraud. Monotheistic religions rely on a simple feat of word art, that takes a subjective idea and with a distraction of attention, replaces it with an illusion of legerdemain to exist objectively, as if a first father god exists outside of humans.

A monotheistic god is a cheat, a subjective way to amuse someone and distract attention from the too often frightening daily show of life and death. Monotheistic religions encourage an individual to act carelessly and foolishly by uncritically accepting the subjective word portrait of a first father god and by so doing an artificial and false sense of security is promoted that often leads to personal failure or even death.

By promoting the subjective idea of a first father god to be objective, monotheistic religions trick and deceive humankind. Monotheism diverts attention away from what can be observed, a triune soul and the environment, to an unobservable metaphorical god. The metaphorical word portrait of a first father god diverts attention away from what animates life internally, a willing triune soul of hunger for food,, sex and reproduction, and aggression that is a continuation of a sea of metaphysical energy particles of the environment. Monotheism diverts attention away from real metaphysical energy to a metaphorical god story. Monotheism is a trick that provides only subjective comfort and zero objective benefit to humankind.

To reliably find what animates life, available evidence must at least be observed if it does not fit into a testable format. To find the animation of life cannot be based on what is unobserved such as faith, belief, and tradition. A theory on the origin of life must be based on observable and confirmed facts. What animates life is a triune soul that can easily be observed. Life is a continuation of what has also only recently been observed to exist, metaphysical energy particles of the environment.

A monotheistic god can be observed to be a subjective metaphor, a story character and is not an objective metaphysical presence. The god only subjectively exists to identify the origin of existence and to provide help and protection for needy humans. To accept the existence of an external monotheistic god is a way to subjectively feel better about living, suffering, and dying. Humans are animated not by an unobservable external monotheistic god but by an observable internal triune soul as urges of hunger for food and water, sex and reproduction, and aggression.

No monotheistic god populates the earth nor an afterlife dimension of energy. Endowed with a biological body from a supportive earth, it returns to the soil during burial or the ashes of cremation. The animating and willing soul returns to what it is a continuation of and what bestows on it a resistance to destruction, a place where it abides for a time, tied as it were to the dimension of energy.

Seductive

The internal idea of a good first father god who exists externally, is a seductive and pragmatic effort using word art to reduce the limitations of life. To talk or write about a first father god is a subjective lure of attention away from now experience, a seductive way to gain some relief albeit brief from the environment, and life and death. The story existence of a first father god is a subjective way to reduce the less conscious and subconscious yearning urges within the midbrain and body, and of getting them to be obedient to the conscious cerebral cortex of the brain and its ideation.

A monotheistic good god is a subjective way to reduce but never entirely escape the yearning internal urges of a triune soul as hunger for food and water, sex and reproduction, and aggression. The monotheistic yearning to find relief from the earth and from life is through what is imagined to have existed before the beginning, a first father god.

Escape from life is to direct attention to what began it. For monotheistic religions, the origin of existence is the subjective and seductive idea of a first father figure, a delusion or mistaken idea that really represents the objective sexual genital reproduction of many real forefathers and mothers.

Offer

All of the foolish and wasted efforts of many adherents expended into the partially successful attempts to convince other humans of the objective existence of a monotheistic god. The offer of a first father who exists to help humans is really a harm as it is a subjective artistic word portrait portrayed as objective. The subjective story provides a false sense of security and protection that does not exist in reality. Many people foolishly elect to save themselves from the willing-like change of the environment, and from individual willing errors of life, by all too uncritically and readily accepting the origin of of existence to be a helping monotheistic god.

In an attempt to find protection in the environment, attention is directed to the past as a way to flee now experience. Fleeing to the past is via a focus of attention on the word art story of a first father, a god who made the environment and the first humans. Subjectively fleeing to the past away from now experience is a psychological maneuver to protect from existent and future harmful experiences.

Since the willing ability of most individuals is limited, many prefer the ideated super willing of a monotheistic god to assist them. Monotheistic authority figures and rulers have known this fact for at least twenty-five hundred years and continue to exploit this weakness of many foolish humans. The wise prefer to explore and cultivate their own individual willing rather than follow those who promote following the fake willing of a monotheistic god. The writings of monotheistic religions are a babble of words, a symptom that blocks human attention from better exploring the conscious self, and the less conscious and subconscious soul. Personal experience is more important than faith and belief in a monotheistic god.

This is borne out by what occurred culturally in the United States during the nineteen-sixties and seventies. During this time, hippies and young people in general, partly tired of social lifestyles, beliefs, and monotheistic traditions, sought out personal experience of body and brain, self and soul. They traveled to India to learn from gurus how to meditate, and many indulged in ingestion of psychedelic drugs as a way of removing limiting cultural concepts such as the tradition of a monotheistic god.

Stability

A monotheistic god is for many people, the great stabilizer of existence. A majority of the earth's population subjectively accept the ideation and artistic word portrait of a monotheistic god to be the great stabilizer of life and death. Without a first father god to provide support, life would be much more prone to destabilizing experiences, and the daily effort of individuals to continue to live would be impaired.

To assert that a monotheistic god is a mere portrait of words, as does the God & Soul Theory, threatens to destabilize the lives of many people who utilize the artistic word art portrait of a first father to subjectively stabilize themselves. A majority of the earth's population appeal to a monotheistic god as a subjective way to remove a myriad of destabilizing anxieties, illnesses, injuries, and despair. Without the existence of a first father god, an individual would be limited to appealing to a minority of stable fellow humans and at risk to appeal to a great many more unstable humans.

Life is not a completely stable condition, it is ever only partially stabilized. Various daily experiences destabilize humans, and life is an effort to stabilize the internal conscious self of the cerebral cortex of the brain, the subconscious soul dynamic of the midbrain and body, and the external environment. Life consists of recurring efforts to manage dualistic situations of stability and remove destabilizing experiences. A monotheistic god is a subjective effort to stabilize an unstable existence. A majority of people prefer a nonvisible first father stabilizer while a minority prefer trial and error learning and pragmatic individual effort to stabilize life situations. Lack of personal health, knowledge, work and financial security, and supportive relationships are existentially destabilizing experiences. Life is easily destabilized and a monotheistic god is identified to be a place to direct attention and prayers for stability in various risk and stressful situations of life.

Two Legends

The word legend is defined as:

"A story passed down from person to person in times past that has not been verified or proven but is often accepted to be factual and true."

The legend of a surviving soul has been mentioned in many stories but omitted in monotheistic stories of a first father god. The legend of the soul has existed much longer than the relatively recent legend of a monotheistic god.

Artifact evidence for the legend of the soul suggests it may have begun circa 100,000 BCE or earlier, perhaps with images of deceased persons glimpsed in dreams. Dream images of the deceased were probably accepted as convincing evidence for survival of the person. It was the Neanderthals who first began to intentionally bury their dead and to place grave goods on or near the body. This began a custom that was later to be followed by modern Homo sapiens.

Later in time, circa 3000 BCE, the soul was accepted to exist in the Aryan and Indo-European tradition. In Hinduism, the soul is known as the *atma* and though not emphasized by name, is also found in Buddhism. The Celts, Greeks and Romans, and European cultures in general accepted the existence of an animating soul. Through the many years, not much has been said of the soul except that it is an ethereal image of the person. Little has been said of what it may consist and what its dynamic might be except to survive physical death.

The legend of a first father began circa 500 BCE in the Middle East tribal tradition of Judaism. The legend later influenced the religions of Christianity and Islam. A monotheistic god is a way to identify the origin of existence, to promote morals, and to rule the population. The first father legend eventually spread to the cultures of Europe and Americas.

The soul is nonexistent in Semitic cultures. In most of Europe the first father legend won out over the soul legend. The Catholic church and secular rulers utilized the first father legend to dominate the under-educated population of Europe. Rulers cannot very well dominate a population with the legend of a surviving soul. For monotheistic authorities and secular rulers, the independent soul does not promote enough dependency as does a first father god. Unfortunately, the legend of a soul, though historically vague, is real, while the legend of a monotheistic first father god is the artistic word art portrait of story.

Autism Spectrum Disorder

The word art of monotheistic religion is a primitive stage of ideation for humankind, and as such can be correctly regarded as a developmental disorder. Having the beneficial findings of science, modern humans are less developmentally afflicted and disabled. Twenty-first century humans who continue to accept monotheistic religious teachings may be diagnosed to present with a mild case of autistic spectrum disorder.

A prominent symptom is turning attention inward, not to experientially observe and comprehend self and soul functions but to attend to a mild fixation on the subjective ideation of a monotheistic god. A further symptom is that monotheistic religious rituals exhibit a repetition of behaviors that contribute to a subjective sense of personal comfort and security when attention is fixed on the ideation of a god.

Advantage

Monotheistic sacerdotalists offer disadvantaged humans an advantage in life, though the offer is subjective and not objective. The advantage of accepting the existence of a monotheistic god's strong willpower and great knowledge, offsets the disadvantage of pitifully weak or ineffective human will power and lack of knowledge. Monotheistic adherents make themselves feel better by subjectively accepting the artistic ruse and advantage of an amazing first father god. An amazing origin is preferred rather than an unamazing lack of knowledge of the origin of existence, and a life consisting of struggle for food and water, sex and reproduction, and aggression.

The character of a monotheistic god is an artistic metaphor for the conscious willing and knowing of the cerebral cortex of the brain. The cerebral cortex is the place of conscious higher knowing, the dwelling place of an ideated first father god, and the knowing of right and wrong, good and bad, by the human conscience. The prototype first two humans of the Genesis story are a metaphor for the disobedient midbrain and body of less conscious and subconscious willing urges of hunger for food and thirst for water, sex and reproduction, and aggression, the unrecognized triune soul.

Edward Conklin

Subjective Story

The biblical story of Genesis is artistic word knowledge that poorly serves to solve the problem of the origin of existence and human willing. In an attempt to solve the problem of existence, a story was subjectively ideated and written about a willing first father who was exaggerated to be a god and who commanded human willing to do good and avoid evil. The Genesis story at once explains the origin of existence and also offers a solution to the problem of human willing.

Circa 500 BCE in the Middle East, humans were ignorant of many things. In retrospect, Genesis word artist scribes subjectively imagined and wrote about a first father god, and were followed through the years by deluded sacerdotalists and the many adherents of monotheistic religions. The much-touted willful sin of separation by the first humans from the god is laid bare for those few who are interested enough to comprehend. The ache and angst of existence, of supposed separation from a monotheistic god, is really a wanting of relief to escape the willing-like change of the environment, the harmful willing of other life forms, and the aggression of fellow humans.

A monotheistic holy day is a time of turning attention from the now time struggle of life to the past and to reconnect with a first father god, said to be the origin of existence. Knowing the beginning of existence to be a god, humans are subjectively made whole. There is no gap of an unknown origin so knowledge of where the environment and life come from, is complete, it is therefore whole or holy. The Catholic holy mass is also wholly a mess of humans assembling in blind faith, belief, and tradition, to worship the subjective ideation and word art of a first father god.

Human Willing

The ideation and artistic word art portrait of a monotheistic god is really a subjective attempt to resolve two kinds of willing within humans.

The primary mode of willing is subconscious functions of midbrain, cells, and organs, and the secondary mode is conscious willing of the cerebral cortex of the brain. The less conscious and subconscious soul, as a continuation of the willing-like non-conscious change of the environment, must for the good of individual survival will for food and water, sex and reproduction, and aggression.

In contrast, the evolved conscious self in the past willed for the good of a monotheistic god as an artistic way of knowing the origin of existence and to obtain care and protection. Humans much more prefer conscious willing of the cerebral cortex of the brain as most important. The ability to consciously ideate was utilized to write a story about a monotheistic god. The conscious cerebral cortex also uses reason, the ability to innovate novel and pragmatic inventions.

While pragmatically useful in the past, the subjective story of a first father god is no longer a useful paradigm with which to explain the origin of existence or to inspire humans to be good and avoid evil. Rather than imagine and will for a subjective artistic word portrait of a first father god, humans must will for what is objectively real and good in life, willing for personal health, knowledge, work and financial security, and supportive relationships.

Alias

The word alias is defined as:

"An assumed or false name given to deceive or conceal a true or legal identity."

The artistic ideated monotheistic first father that is idolized to be a god, is an alias for many biological ancestor fathers who along with mothers have biologically reproduced humankind. Monotheistic religion most likely began with oral folk stories, and later on, was elaborated on by word artist scribes who mistakenly extrapolated from a succession of many forefathers to a single first father and idolized it to be a marvelous god.

The alias portrayed in monotheistic word art story has been advocated through the years by many sacerdotalists to direct the attention of and to deceive many people to accept the mistake or delusion that is monotheistic religion.

A monotheistic god is an alias fabricated by word artists in an effort intended to identify an unknown origin, and from where, what, and how the environment and life has come to exist. The first father god of monotheism is an artistic misidentification that fails to correctly identify energy particles of the environment to be the origin of existence. The external monotheistic willing god is a contrived alias that ignores an internal willing soul to be a continuation of energy particles of the environment, and is therefore resistant to destruction. For monotheistic religions, only the god is deemed resistant to destruction.

Eyes

A popular saying is, "The eyes are the windows of the soul." This is a misnomer as the eyes are more accurately the windows of the self, the civilized and cultured part of an individual. In contrast, the soul is a lineage that seeks to survive the fray of life and death on the blood-soaked earth. If the soul can truly be glimpsed through the window-like eyes, it would be observed and comprehended to be a triune function of hunger for food and water, sex and reproduction, and aggression.

Atheism

The English word atheism means without a god (Greek a, without, *theos*, god). The view that a monotheistic god does not exist is known as atheism. In the Middle East and western countries, few can live without a monotheistic god. Many people needing help subjectively accept on faith and tradition the existence of a first father. It is easier for many people to find solace in the ideation of a monotheistic god rather than with fellow humans. A god does not argue while humans seldom cease from conflict of verbal arguments and physical fights.

A curious individual must examine the putative existence of a monotheistic god with eyes wide open rather than shut tightly in subjective faith and belief in a blind imitative tradition. Yet, to question the existence of a monotheistic god is traditionally regarded as evil. Not to be under the protection of a good first father god is to be with what is not good, and it must therefore be bad. If an individual is not for or with a first father god, then the person is with either a known or unknown bad influence. Those who accept the imaginal ideation of a first father god, think of themselves as good and better. For followers of monotheistic religions, the individuals who do not accept the word art story of a monotheistic god are not good and are by perforce bad.

Without a god or gods, there would have been no knowledge of the beginning of existence or of how the environment or humans got to be how they are. For the older cultures of the Hindus, Greeks, Sumerians, and Egyptians, to be without gods is to be without an explanation for events. The gods and goddesses were acceptable knowledge bases in lieu of nonexistent observing and testing of science.

In contrast to the deluding distortion of monotheism, atheism is to be admired for its good mental hygiene, self-reliance, and clear-sightedness that few manage to reach in a lifetime. Atheism is really noble and good and is an absence of the subjective crutch and the folk tale of a first father god. To be without a monotheistic god demonstrates maturity and responsibility. Atheists usually practice good mental hygiene and are annoyed and often irritated by the subjective delusion, the mistaken idea of a monotheistic first father god. Good atheists must overlook and pity the weaknesses of their less perceptive majority fellow humans. However, the existential task for atheists remains the same as for monotheists, as neither accept the existence of a soul.

Atheists do not accept that a soul exists. Neither do monotheist religions as adherents *en masse* look forward to a body resurrection performed by a first father god.

If both atheists and monotheists investigate its phenomenal existence, both orientations will eventually be persuaded by the real observable and experiential evidence of a dynamic triune soul that as a continuation of energy is resistant to destruction.

Let those who are able, discard the out of date simple ideation and word artistry of a first father god genealogy. Let he or she be proud of atheism, of living without the subjective ideational crutch of a monotheistic god. Let the noble atheist also know he or she has an animating triune soul that urgingly wills for food and water, sex and reproduction, and aggression, and that as a continuation of energy particles of the real universe is resistant to destruction. Further know that following death, the animating soul will enter into another dimension of energy, and may also return from that place to exist again on the earth. What an individual has ably made of life will be sufficient and just.

Superstition

It has been a long climb for evolving humans to free themselves from a plethora of superstitions. A few examples include, the sun revolves around a flat earth that is the center of the universe, mermaids exist, and the number thirteen and black cats are bad luck. Many other superstitions have only slowly been discarded on the laborious human ascent to what is proven to be true by the empirical sciences of physics, biology, anthropology, archaeology, medicine, and psychology.

Having survived to the twenty-first century, humankind has only recently arrived near a summit and vantage point that can clearly surveil the long-trusted knowledge of an objective monotheistic god to be a subjective superstition. Like so many previous superstitions, the subjective word art portrait of a first father is now in tatters from long overuse. Monotheistic religions are even now being discarded to the refuge pile of other moribund beliefs and traditions, and are track to be replaced with the much more reliable and valuable findings of science.

The God & Soul Theory calls for an end to the use of the subjective artistic word portrait of a monotheistic god. The concept can only continue to be utilized for as long as a first father is not comprehended to exist objectively but is a subjective spoken and written word art portrait, a folk way to display the origin of existence, and to provide those in need with care and protection.

Both a god and a soul exist inside of humans. The first father god exists within the cerebral cortex as a subjective ideation that is spoken and written about. In contrast, the soul is a real objective dynamic function of midbrain and body, a triune urging of hunger for food and water, sex and reproduction, and aggression.

Monotheistic religions display a double ignorance. Not only do they superstitiously insist that a first father god exists objectively but they also suffer from the failure and crippling ignorance of not recognizing a real animating soul that as a continuation of energy is resistant to destruction. The God & Soul Theory makes a call for cognitive clarity by directing and training human attention to observation and comprehension of a real self and soul within that is a continuation of a real environment. When the conscious self comprehends the less conscious and subconscious soul to be a continuation of the environment, then can be discarded the superstitious word art portrait of a monotheistic god.

Monotheistic religions represent a degenerate line of thinking, a dead-end category of word art that will soon be accepted to be artistic and not realistic. No convincing objective evidence for the existence of a monotheistic god exists, aside from mention of an inclusion in an insurance policy that with the use of words only, attribute some weather or environmental events to be evidence of an "act of god." This mention is the result of historical superstition and tradition.

Frequently in story, when there is mention of a monotheistic god, weather and geological events often occur as evidence for the existence of the first father that causes them to happen. (Matthew 27: 51)

The willing-like changes of the environment have long been attributed to various gods. This tendency is a habit pattern begun by oral folk tales and eventually written by skilled word artist scribes. Geological and weather events are often cited as evidence for the existence of a god that causes environmental events. Only geological events are real and objective while theological word art is completely subjective and false. A monotheistic god is a subjective work of spoken and written word art that is significant only as a primitive and artistic way to easily identify the beginning of the environment and life, and the genealogy of humans. The word god is but a subjective idea and empty echo that resounds only in the cerebral cortex of a human head.

The objective existence of a first father cannot be convincingly demonstrated through the testament words of prophetic individuals who claim interaction with a monotheistic god, the subjective words of mystics, or the testing of empirical science. A first father god occurs only as a subjective notion in the cerebral cortex of the brain and nowhere else, and evidence for this can only be presented in philosophical and psychological argument. The average discerning reader or listener, will then tend to be either convinced or unconvinced.

Superstition and magical thinking are deemed to be primitive by today's standards of monotheistic religion and science. In modern times, it is considered much more civilized and advanced to accept the artistic word portrait of a monotheistic god. Yet in contrast with modern science, monotheism and its god story is a primitive stage for humankind. The next stage of advanced thinking for humankind will consist of a further in-depth psychological exploration of a monotheistic god to be a subjective metaphor, and better comprehension of the conscious self and subconscious soul.

Both ways of thinking, a monotheistic god and exploration of self and soul developed circa 500 BCE. Monotheism, the worship of a first father god developed in the Judaic culture of Israel, eventually developing into Christianity, and Islam, and spread to the rest of the Middle East and Europe.

Exploration of the conscious self and subconscious soul began in India circa 3200 BCE with the Hindu practice of yoga and meditation, and reached its zenith in the experiential teachings of Buddha circa 623-543 BCE.

The simplistic teaching of a monotheistic god has in the past and continues to appeal widely to many individuals today. The time has arrived to release the fear-ridden adherence to the tradition of a monotheistic god. Utilizing the basic criterion of science, the transition to meditative observation of the conscious self and the soul can no longer be avoided. To continue to adhere to monotheistic religions will continue to smother the uplifting truth of self and soul exploration and clarity of comprehension.

Meditation is the training of conscious attention to become a consummate observer. Few humans have lived in the past, and are now living whose abiding interest is to focus conscious attention and train to comprehend the individual twin dynamic of self and soul. Human willing effort to accomplish is limited and often only partially effective. Then what must be relied upon is "grace" but not as defined by monotheistic religions to be an unmerited gift from a fatherly god. Real grace occurs when an individual observes and accepts their existence to be a lesser conscious self and a greater animating less conscious and subconscious soul. Grace occurs when the human soul is comprehended and accepted to be a real continuation of the all-powerful nonconscious cause and effect sea of energy particles that constitute the reality of gaseous, liquid, and material conditions of the environment.

Rejecting what is subjective, metaphorical, and unreal, and by accepting only what can be observed and comprehended to be real, an individual has then achieved a state of merited grace. By so doing, an individual will develop a true sense of propriety and consideration for others, and a pleasing sense of accomplishment. The person will exhibit a thankfulness for inspiration from others and from their own efforts in glimpsing a shared continuation of existence that evokes a true disposition to kindness and compassion.

Edward Conklin

Fresh Water

Drawing fresh cool water from a deep well is seldom done during modern times. Most get their chemical treated water from a widespread system of surface reservoirs, shared shallow laid pipes, and the terminal end of a spigot. Only a few much more prefer the cool, clear, and pure refreshing well water of the depths, springing up from the unseen underground seams and rivulets collecting from the high places, having flowed down below along the purifying porous and solid bedrock deep beneath the surface.

www.ingramcontent.com/pod-product-compliance
Lightning Source LLC
Chambersburg PA
CBHW071425160426
43195CB00013B/1812